MznLnx

Missing Links Exam Preps

Exam Prep for

Precalculus

Beecher, Penna, Bittinger, 2nd Edition

The MznLnx Exam Prep is your link from the texbook and lecture to your exams.
The MznLnx Exam Preps are unauthorized and comprehensive reviews of your textbooks.

All material provided by MznLnx and Rico Publications (c) 2010
Textbook publishers and textbook authors do not particpate in or contribute to these reviews.

MznLnx

Rico Publications

Exam Prep for Precalculus
2nd Edition
Beecher, Penna, Bittinger

Publisher: Raymond Houge
Assistant Editor: Michael Rouger
Text and Cover Designer: Lisa Buckner
Marketing Manager: Sara Swagger
Project Manager, Editorial Production: Jerry Emerson
Art Director: Vernon Lowerui

Product Manager: Dave Mason
Editorial Assitant: Rachel Guzmanji
Pedagogy: Debra Long
Cover Image: Jim Reed/Getty Images
Text and Cover Printer: City Printing, Inc.
Compositor: Media Mix, Inc.

(c) 2010 Rico Publications
ALL RIGHTS RESERVED. No part of this work covered by the copyright may be reproduced or used in any form or by an means--graphic, electronic, or mechanical, including photocopying, recording, taping, Web distribution, information storage, and retrieval systems, or in any other manner--without the written permission of the publisher.

Printed in the United States
ISBN:

For more information about our products, contact us at:
Dave.Mason@RicoPublications.com

For permission to use material from this text or product, submit a request online to:
Dave.Mason@RicoPublications.com

Contents

CHAPTER 1
Basic Concepts of Algebra — 1

CHAPTER 2
Graphs, Functions, and Models — 17

CHAPTER 3
Functions, Equations, and Inequalities — 36

CHAPTER 4
Polynomialand Rational Functions — 47

CHAPTER 5
Exponential andLogarithmic Functions — 57

CHAPTER 6
The Trigonometric Functions — 67

CHAPTER 7
Trigonometric Identities, Inverse Functions, and Equations — 75

CHAPTER 8
Applications of Trigonometry — 79

CHAPTER 9
Systems of Equations and Matrices — 91

CHAPTER 10
Conic Sections — 106

CHAPTER 11
Sequences, Series, and Combinatorics — 113

ANSWER KEY — 128

TO THE STUDENT

COMPREHENSIVE

The *MznLnx* Exam Prep series is designed to help you pass your exams. Editors at MznLnx review your textbooks and then prepare these practice exams to help you master the textbook material. Unlike study guides, workbooks, and practice tests provided by the texbook publisher and textbook authors, *MznLnx* gives you **all** of the material in each chapter in exam form, not just samples, so you can be sure to nail your exam.

MECHANICAL

The MznLnx Exam Prep series creates exams that will help you learn the subject matter as well as test you on your understanding. Each question is designed to help you master the concept. Just working through the exams, you gain an understanding of the subject--its a simple mechanical process that produces success.

INTEGRATED STUDY GUIDE AND REVIEW

MznLnx is not just a set of exams designed to test you, its also a comprehensive review of the subject content. Each exam question is also a review of the concept, making sure that you will get the answer correct without having to go to other sources of material. You learn as you go! Its the easiest way to pass an exam.

HUMOR

Studying can be tedious and dry. MznLnx's instructional design includes moderate humor within the exam questions on occassion, to break the tedium and revitalize the brain

Chapter 1. Basic Concepts of Algebra

1. The _____ are the set of numbers consisting of the natural numbers including 0 and their negatives. They are numbers that can be written without a fractional or decimal component, and fall within the set {... −2, −1, 0, 1, 2, ...}.
    a. A chemical equation
    b. A Mathematical Theory of Communication
    c. A posteriori
    d. Integers

2. In mathematics, a _____ can mean either an element of the set {1, 2, 3, ...} or an element of the set {0, 1, 2, 3, ...}. The latter is especially preferred in mathematical logic, set theory, and computer science.

    _____s have two main purposes: they can be used for counting, and they can be used for ordering.

    a. Strong partition cardinal
    b. Suslin cardinal
    c. Cardinal numbers
    d. Natural number

3. In mathematics, a _____ is a number which can be expressed as a ratio of two integers. Non-integer _____s are usually written as the vulgar fraction $\frac{a}{b}$, where b is not zero. a is called the numerator, and b the denominator.
    a. Pre-algebra
    b. Tally marks
    c. Minkowski distance
    d. Rational number

4. In mathematics, the _____s may be described informally in several different ways. The _____s include both rational numbers, such as 42 and −23/129, and irrational numbers, such as pi and the square root of two; or, a _____ can be given by an infinite decimal representation, such as 2.4871773339...., where the digits continue in some way; or, the _____s may be thought of as points on an infinitely long number line.

    These descriptions of the _____s, while intuitively accessible, are not sufficiently rigorous for the purposes of pure mathematics.

    a. Tally marks
    b. Pre-algebra
    c. Minkowski distance
    d. Real number

5. In mathematics, a _____ can mean either an element of the set {1, 2, 3, ...} (i.e the positive integers) or an element of the set {0, 1, 2, 3, ...} (i.e. the non-negative integers).
    a. FISH
    b. Whole number
    c. Bounded
    d. Degrees of freedom

6. In elementary algebra, a _____ is a polynomial with two terms: the sum of two monomials. It is the simplest kind of polynomial except for a monomial.

    The _____ $a^2 - b^2$ can be factored as the product of two other _____s:

    $a^2 - b^2$.

    The product of a pair of linear _____s a x + b and c x + d is:

    $2 + x + bd$.

A _____ raised to the nth power, represented as

$$\binom{n}{}$$

can be expanded by means of the _____ theorem or, equivalently, using Pascal's triangle.

a. Cylindrical algebraic decomposition
b. Real structure
c. Rational root theorem
d. Binomial

7. In mathematics, the _____ $\binom{n}{k}$ is the coefficient of the x^k term in the polynomial expansion of the binomial power ^{n}.

In combinatorics, $\binom{n}{k}$ is interpreted as the number of k-element subsets of an n-element set, that is the number of ways that k things can be 'chosen' from a set of n things. Hence, $\binom{n}{k}$ is often read as 'n choose k' and called the choose function of n and k.

a. Dyson conjecture
b. Rule of product
c. Binomial coefficient
d. Symbolic combinatorics

8. In mathematics, a _____ is a constant multiplicative factor of a certain object. For example, in the expression $9x^2$, the _____ of x^2 is 9.

The object can be such things as a variable, a vector, a function, etc.

a. Fibonacci polynomials
b. Stability radius
c. Multivariate division algorithm
d. Coefficient

9. In mathematics, an _____ or member of a set is any one of the distinct objects that make up that set.

Writing A = {1,2,3,4}, means that the _____s of the set A are the numbers 1, 2, 3 and 4. Groups of _____s of A, for example {1,2}, are subsets of A.

a. Universal code
b. Ideal
c. Order
d. Element

10. In mathematics, an inequality is a statement about the relative size or order of two objects. For example 14 > 10, or 14 is _____ 10. The notation a > b means that a is _____ b and 'a' would be to the right of 'b' on a number line.

a. Greater than
b. Cauchy-Schwarz inequality
c. FKG inequality
d. Minkowski inequality

Chapter 1. Basic Concepts of Algebra

11. In mathematics, a _____ is a set of real numbers with the property that any number that lies between two numbers in the set is also included in the set. For example, the set of all numbers x satisfying $0 \leq x \leq 1$ is an _____ which contains 0 and 1, as well as all numbers between them. Other examples of _____s are the set of all real numbers $\mathbb{R}$, the set of all positive real numbers, and the empty set.
   a. Interval
   b. Ideal
   c. Annihilator
   d. Order

12. _____ is the notation in which permitted values for a variable are expressed as ranging over a certain interval; "5 < x < 9" is an example of the application of _____.
   a. Infinity
   b. Interval notation
   c. A Mathematical Theory of Communication
   d. Implicit differentiation

13. In mathematics, a _____ is a picture of a straight line in which the integers are shown as specially-marked points evenly spaced on the line. Although this image only shows the integers from -9 to 9, the line includes all real numbers, continuing 'forever' in each direction. It is often used as an aid in teaching simple addition and subtraction, especially involving negative numbers.
   a. Real number
   b. Point plotting
   c. Number system
   d. Number line

14. In mathematics, an _____ in the sense of ring theory is a subring $\mathcal{O}$ of a ring R that satisfies the conditions

   1. R is a ring which is a finite-dimensional algebra over the rational number field $\mathbb{Q}$
   2. $\mathcal{O}$ spans R over $\mathbb{Q}$, so that $\mathbb{Q}\mathcal{O} = R$, and
   3. $\mathcal{O}$ is a lattice in R.

The third condition can be stated more accurately, in terms of the extension of scalars of R to the real numbers, embedding R in a real vector space. In less formal terms, additively $\mathcal{O}$ should be a free abelian group generated by a basis for R over $\mathbb{Q}$.

The leading example is the case where R is a number field K and $\mathcal{O}$ is its ring of integers. In algebraic number theory there are examples for any K other than the rational field of proper subrings of the ring of integers that are also _____s.

   a. Efficiency
   b. Algebraic
   c. Annihilator
   d. Order

15. In mathematics, especially in set theory, a set A is a _____ of a set B if A is 'contained' inside B. Notice that A and B may coincide. The relationship of one set being a _____ of another is called inclusion.
   a. Set of all sets
   b. Cartesian product
   c. Horizontal line test
   d. Subset

16. In mathematics, especially in the area of abstract algebra known as ring theory, a _____ is a ring with 0 ≠ 1 such that ab = 0 implies that either a = 0 or b = 0. That is, it is a nontrivial ring without left or right zero divisors. A commutative _____ is called an integral _____.

Chapter 1. Basic Concepts of Algebra

a. Left primitive ring
b. Modular representation theory
c. Simple ring
d. Domain

17. In mathematics the _____ of a set which is equipped with the operation of addition is an element which, when added to any element x in the set, yields x. One of the most familiar additive identities is the number 0 from elementary mathematics, but additive identities occur in other mathematical structures where addition is defined, such as in groups and rings.

- The _____ familiar from elementary mathematics is zero, denoted 0. For example,

    5 + 0 = 5 = 0 + 5.

- In the natural numbers N and all of its supersets, the _____ is 0. Thus for any one of these numbers n,

    n + 0 = n = 0 + n.

Let N be a set which is closed under the operation of addition, denoted +. An _____ for N is any element e such that for any element n in N,

e + n = n = n + e.

a. Algebraically independent
b. Additive identity
c. Unique factorization domain
d. Unit ring

18. In mathematics, the _____ of a number n is the number that, when added to n, yields zero. The _____ of n is denoted −n. For example, 7 is −7, because 7 + (−7) = 0, and the _____ of −0.3 is 0.3, because −0.3 + 0.3 = 0.
a. Additive inverse
b. Algebraic structure
c. Arity
d. Associativity

19. In mathematics, _____ is a property that a binary operation can have. It means that, within an expression containing two or more of the same associative operators in a row, the order that the operations are performed does not matter as long as the sequence of the operands is not changed. That is, rearranging the parentheses in such an expression will not change its value.
a. Idempotence
b. Algebraically closed
c. Unital
d. Associativity

20. In mathematics, and in particular in abstract algebra, distributivity is a property of binary operations that generalises the _____ law from elementary algebra.
a. Permutation
b. General linear group
c. Closure with a twist
d. Distributive

21. _____ is the mathematical operation of scaling one number by another. It is one of the four basic operations in elementary arithmetic.

_____ is defined for whole numbers in terms of repeated addition; for example, 4 multiplied by 3 can be calculated by adding 3 copies of 4 together:

$$4 + 4 + 4 = 12.$$

_____ of rational numbers and real numbers is defined by systematic generalization of this basic idea.

a. Highest common factor
c. Least common multiple
b. The number 0 is even.
d. Multiplication

22. In mathematics, a _____ for a number x, denoted by $1/x$ or x^{-1}, is a number which when multiplied by x yields the multiplicative identity, 1. The _____ of x is also called the reciprocal of x. The _____ of a fraction p/q is q/p.
   a. Hyperbolic function
   b. Double exponential
   c. Golden function
   d. Multiplicative inverse

23. The _____ is a rule which states that when you add or multiply numbers, changing the order doesn't change the result.
   a. Semigroupoid
   b. Coimage
   c. Commutative law
   d. Conditional event algebra

24. In mathematics, the term _____ has several different important meanings:

- An _____ is an equality that remains true regardless of the values of any variables that appear within it, to distinguish it from an equality which is true under more particular conditions. For this, the 'triple bar' symbol ≡ is sometimes used.
- In algebra, an _____ or _____ element of a set S with a binary operation Â· is an element e that, when combined with any element x of S, produces that same x. That is, eÂ·x = xÂ·e = x for all x in S.
    - The _____ function from a set S to itself, often denoted id or id_S, s the function such that i = x for all x in S. This function serves as the _____ element in the set of all functions from S to itself with respect to function composition.
    - In linear algebra, the _____ matrix of size n is the n-by-n square matrix with ones on the main diagonal and zeros elsewhere. This matrix serves as the _____ with respect to matrix multiplication.

A common example of the first meaning is the trigonometric _____

$$\sin^2 \theta + \cos^2 \theta = 1$$

which is true for all real values of θ, as opposed to

$$\cos \theta = 1,$$

which is true only for some values of θ, not all. For example, the latter equation is true when $\theta = 0$, false when $\theta = 2$

The concepts of 'additive _____' and 'multiplicative _____' are central to the Peano axioms. The number 0 is the 'additive _____' for integers, real numbers, and complex numbers. For the real numbers, for all $a \in \mathbb{R}$,

$$0 + a = a,$$

$$a + 0 = a,$$ and

$$0 + 0 = 0.$$

Similarly, The number 1 is the 'multiplicative _____' for integers, real numbers, and complex numbers.

   a. Intersection   b. ARIA
   c. Action   d. Identity

25. _____ is a branch of mathematics which focuses on the study of matrices. Initially a sub-branch of linear algebra, it has grown to cover subjects related to graph theory, algebra, combinatorics, and statistics as well.

The term matrix was first coined in 1848 by J.J. Sylvester as a name of an array of numbers.

   a. Pairing   b. Matrix theory
   c. Segre classification   d. Semi-simple operators

26. In mathematics, a _____ is a rectangular table of elements, which may be numbers or, more generally, any abstract quantities that can be added and multiplied. Matrices are used to describe linear equations, keep track of the coefficients of linear transformations and to record data that depend on multiple parameters. Matrices are described by the field of _____ theory.

   a. Double counting   b. Compression
   c. Coherent   d. Matrix

27. In mathematics, the _____ of a real number is its numerical value without regard to its sign. So, for example, 3 is the _____ of both 3 and −3.

The _____ of a number a is denoted by $|\,a\,|$.

Generalizations of the _____ for real numbers occur in a wide variety of mathematical settings.

   a. A Mathematical Theory of Communication   b. Absolute value
   c. Area hyperbolic functions   d. A chemical equation

28. In mathematics, a _____ on a fiber bundle is a device that defines a notion of parallel transport on the bundle; that is, a way to 'connect' or identify fibers over nearby points. If the fiber bundle is a vector bundle, then the notion of parallel transport is required to be linear. Such a _____ is equivalently specified by a covariant derivative, which is an operator that can differentiate sections of that bundle along tangent directions in the base manifold.

Chapter 1. Basic Concepts of Algebra

a. Connectivity
b. 120-cell
c. Connection
d. 1-center problem

29. A _____ typically refers to a class of handheld calculators that are capable of plotting graphs, solving simultaneous equations, and performing numerous other tasks with variables. Most popular _____s are also programmable, allowing the user to create customized programs, typically for scientific/engineering and education applications. Due to their large displays intended for graphing, they can also accommodate several lines of text and calculations at a time.

a. Genus
b. Support vector machines
c. Bump mapping
d. Graphing calculator

30. A _____ is a device for performing mathematical calculations, distinguished from a computer by having a limited problem solving ability and an interface optimized for interactive calculation rather than programming. _____s can be hardware or software, and mechanical or electronic, and are often built into devices such as PDAs or mobile phones.

Modern electronic _____s are generally small, digital, and usually inexpensive.

a. 120-cell
b. 2-3 heap
c. 1-center problem
d. Calculator

31. In mathematics and in the sciences, a _____ (plural: _____e, formulæ or _____s) is a concise way of expressing information symbolically (as in a mathematical or chemical _____), or a general relationship between quantities. One of many famous _____e is Albert Einstein's $E = mc^2$ (see special relativity

In mathematics, a _____ is a key to solve an equation with variables. For example, the problem of determining the volume of a sphere is one that requires a significant amount of integral calculus to solve.

a. 120-cell
b. Formula
c. 1-center problem
d. 2-3 heap

32. In mathematics, a _____ is an expression constructed from variables and constants, using the operations of addition, subtraction, multiplication, and constant non-negative whole number exponents. For example, $x^2 - 4x + 7$ is a _____, but $x^2 - 4/x + 7x^{3/2}$ is not, because its second term involves division by the variable x and also because its third term contains an exponent that is not a whole number.

_____s are one of the most important concepts in algebra and throughout mathematics and science.

a. Semifield
b. Coimage
c. Group extension
d. Polynomial

33. The mathematical concept of a _____ expresses the intuitive idea of deterministic dependence between two quantities, one of which is viewed as primary and the other as secondary. A _____ then is a way to associate a unique output for each input of a specified type, for example, a real number or an element of a given set.

a. Going up
b. Grill
c. Function
d. Coherent

34. In mathematics and computer science, _____ (also base-16, hexa or base, of 16. It uses sixteen distinct symbols, most often the symbols 0-9 to represent values zero to nine, and A, B, C, D, E, F (or a through f) to represent values ten to fifteen.

Its primary use is as a human friendly representation of binary coded values, so it is often used in digital electronics and computer engineering.

a. Tetradecimal
b. Radix
c. Factoradic
d. Hexadecimal

35. Exponentiation is a mathematical operation, written a^n, involving two numbers, the base a and the _____ n. When n is a positive integer, exponentiation corresponds to repeated multiplication:

$$a^n = \underbrace{a \times \cdots \times a}_{n},$$

just as multiplication by a positive integer corresponds to repeated addition:

$$a \times n = \underbrace{a + \cdots + a}_{n}.$$

The _____ is usually shown as a superscript to the right of the base. The exponentiation a^n can be read as: a raised to the n-th power, a raised to the power [of] n or possibly a raised to the _____ [of] n, or more briefly: a to the n-th power or a to the power [of] n, or even more briefly: a to the n.

a. Exponent
b. Exponentiating by squaring
c. Exponential sum
d. Exponential tree

36. Scientific notation, also sometimes known as standard form or as _____, is a way of writing numbers that accommodates values too large or small to be conveniently written in standard decimal notation. Scientific notation has a number of useful properties and is often favored by scientists, mathematicians and engineers, who work with such numbers.

In scientific notation, numbers are written in the form:

$$a \times 10^b$$

a. A posteriori
b. A chemical equation
c. A Mathematical Theory of Communication
d. Exponential Notation

37. This article will state and prove the _____ for differentiation, and then use it to prove these two formulas.

The _____ for differentiation states that for every natural number n, the derivative of $f(x) = x^n$ is $f'(x) = nx^{n-1}$, that is,

$$(x^n)' = nx^{n-1}.$$

The _____ for integration

$$\int x^n \, dx = \frac{x^{n+1}}{n+1} + C$$

for natural n is then an easy consequence. One just needs to take the derivative of this equality and use the _____ and linearity of differentiation on the right-hand side.

a. Periodic function
c. Standard part function
b. Functional integration
d. Power rule

38. The _____ governs the differentiation of products of differentiable functions.
   a. 1-center problem
   c. Reciprocal Rule
   b. 120-cell
   d. Product rule

39. In mathematics, a _____ is the end result of a division problem. It can also be expressed as the number of times the divisor divides into the dividend.
   a. Notation
   c. Quotient
   b. Limiting
   d. Marginal cost

40. In mathematics, the _____s are an extension of the real numbers obtained by adjoining an imaginary unit, denoted i, which satisfies:

$$i^2 = -1.$$

Every _____ can be written in the form a + bi, where a and b are real numbers called the real part and the imaginary part of the _____, respectively.

_____s are a field, and thus have addition, subtraction, multiplication, and division operations. These operations extend the corresponding operations on real numbers, although with a number of additional elegant and useful properties, e.g., negative real numbers can be obtained by squaring _____s.

a. 1-center problem
c. Real part
b. 120-cell
d. Complex number

Chapter 1. Basic Concepts of Algebra

41. _____, also sometimes known as standard form or as exponential notation, is a way of writing numbers that accommodates values too large or small to be conveniently written in standard decimal notation. _____ has a number of useful properties and is often favored by scientists, mathematicians and engineers, who work with such numbers.

In _____, numbers are written in the form:

$$a \times 10^b$$

a. Radix point
b. Leading zero
c. 1-center problem
d. Scientific notation

42. The _____ is a unit of plane angle, equal to 180/π degrees, or about 57.2958 degrees. It is the standard unit of angular measurement in all areas of mathematics beyond the elementary level.

The _____ is represented by the symbol 'rad' or, more rarely, by the superscript c.

a. RADIAN
b. 2-3 heap
c. 1-center problem
d. 120-cell

43. In mathematics, a _____ of a set X is a collection of sets such that X is a subset of the union of sets in the collection. In symbols, if

$$C = \{U_\alpha : \alpha \in A\}$$

is an indexed family of sets U_α, then C is a _____ of X if

$$X \subseteq \bigcup_{\alpha \in A} U_\alpha$$

_____s are commonly used in the context of topology. If the set X is a topological space, then a _____ C of X is a collection of subsets U_α of X whose union is the whole space X.

a. Contractible space
b. Generalised metric
c. Manifold
d. Cover

44. In statistics, the _____ is the value that occurs the most frequently in a data set or a probability distribution. In some fields, notably education, sample data are often called scores, and the sample _____ is known as the modal score.

Like the statistical mean and the median, the _____ is a way of capturing important information about a random variable or a population in a single quantity.

Chapter 1. Basic Concepts of Algebra

a. Field
b. Function
c. Deltoid
d. Mode

45. _____ is the concept of adding accumulated interest back to the principal, so that interest is earned on interest from that moment on. The act of declaring interest to be principal is called compounding. A loan, for example, may have its interest compounded every month: in this case, a loan with $100 principal and 1% interest per month would have a balance of $101 at the end of the first month.

a. Net interest margin
b. Retained interest
c. Compound interest
d. Net interest margin securities

46. _____ is a fee, paid on borrowed capital. Assets lent include money, shares, consumer goods through hire purchase, major assets such as aircraft, and even entire factories in finance lease arrangements. The _____ is calculated upon the value of the assets in the same manner as upon money.

a. Interest sensitivity gap
b. Interest expense
c. A Mathematical Theory of Communication
d. Interest

47. In algebra and computer programming, when a number or expression is both preceded and followed by a binary operation, a rule is required for which operation should be applied first; this rule is known as an _____ . From the earliest use of mathematical notation, multiplication took precedence over addition, whichever side of a number it appeared on. Thus 3 + 4 × 5 = 5 × 4 + 3 = 23.

a. Isomorphism class
b. Identity element
c. Order of operations
d. Algebraic K-theory

48. In mathematics, the _____ of a polynomial is the term of degree 0. For example, in the polynomial

$$X^3 + 2X + 3$$

over the variable X, the _____ is 3. Here, the _____ is given by a numeral, but it may also be specified by a letter that is a parameter rather than a variable, as in the polynomial

$$ax^2 + bx + c,$$

in the variable x, where a, b, and c are parameters so that c is the _____.

a. Stability radius
b. Sheffer sequence
c. Jacobian conjecture
d. Constant term

49. In mathematics, the word _____ means two different things in the context of polynomials:

- The first meaning is a product of powers of variables, or formally any value obtained from 1 by finitely many multiplications by a variable. If only a single variable x is considered this means that any _____ is either 1 or a power x^n of x, with n a positive integer. If several variables are considered, say, x, y, z, then each can be given an exponent, so that any _____ is of the form $x^a y^b z^c$ with a,b,c nonnegative integers.
- The second meaning of _____ includes _____s in the first sense, but also allows multiplication by any constant, so that $-7x^5$ and $4yz^{13}$ are also considered to be _____s.

With either definition, the set of _____s is a subset of all polynomials that is closed under multiplication.

a. Homogeneous polynomial
b. Power sum symmetric polynomial
c. Monomial
d. Diagonal form

50. The _____ fallacy is an informal fallacy. It ascribes cause where none exists. The flaw is failing to account for natural fluctuations.

a. Regression
b. Differential
c. Degrees of freedom
d. Depth

51. In linear algebra, two n-by-n matrices A and B over the field K are called _____ if there exists an invertible n-by-n matrix P over K such that

$$P^{-1}AP = B.$$

One of the meanings of the term similarity transformation is such a transformation of a matrix A into a matrix B.

Similarity is an equivalence relation on the space of square matrices.

_____ matrices share many properties:

- rank
- determinant
- trace
- eigenvalues
- characteristic polynomial
- minimal polynomial
- elementary divisors

There are two reasons for these facts:

- two _____ matrices can be thought of as describing the same linear map, but with respect to different bases
- the map $X \mapsto P^{-1}XP$ is an automorphism of the associative algebra of all n-by-n matrices, as the one-object case of the above category of all matrices.

Because of this, for a given matrix A, one is interested in finding a simple 'normal form' B which is _____ to A -- the study of A then reduces to the study of the simpler matrix B.

a. Coherence
b. Similar
c. Dense
d. Blinding

52. In elementary algebra, a _____ is a polynomial consisting of three terms; in other words, a _____ is the sum of three monomials. It can be factored using simple steps

In linguistics, a _____ is a fixed expression which is made from three words; e.g. 'lights, camera, action', 'signed, sealed, delivered'.

   a. Recurrence relation
   c. Relation algebra
   b. Symmetric difference
   d. Trinomial

53. In mathematics, an arithmetic progression or _____ is a sequence of numbers such that the difference of any two successive members of the sequence is a constant. For instance, the sequence 3, 5, 7, 9, 11, 13... is an arithmetic progression with common difference 2.
   a. Edgeworth series
   c. Alternating series test
   b. Eisenstein series
   d. Arithmetic sequence

54. In mathematics, a _____ is a natural number which has exactly two distinct natural number divisors: 1 and itself. An infinitude of _____s exists, as demonstrated by Euclid around 300 BC. The first twenty-five _____s are:

   2, 3, 5, 7, 11, 13, 17, 19, 23, 29, 31, 37, 41, 43, 47, 53, 59, 61, 67, 71, 73, 79, 83, 89, 97.

   a. Pronic number
   c. Highly composite number
   b. Prime number
   d. Perrin number

55. In game theory, a player's _____ in a game is a complete plan of action for whatever situation might arise; this fully determines the player's behaviour. A player's _____ will determine the action the player will take at any stage of the game, for every possible history of play up to that stage.

A _____ profile is a set of strategies for each player which fully specifies all actions in a game.

   a. Sir Philip Sidney game
   c. Correlated equilibrium
   b. Matching pennies
   d. Strategy

56. In the study of metric spaces in mathematics, there are various notions of two metrics on the same underlying space being 'the same', or _____.

In the following, M will denote a non-empty set and d_1 and d_2 will denote two metrics on M.

The two metrics d_1 and d_2 are said to be topologically _____ if they generate the same topology on M.

   a. A posteriori
   c. A chemical equation
   b. A Mathematical Theory of Communication
   d. Equivalent

57. In mathematics, the _____ or least common denominator is the least common multiple of the denominators of a set of vulgar fractions. It is the smallest positive integer that is a multiple of the denominators. For instance, the _____ of

$$\left\{\frac{5}{12}, \frac{11}{18}\right\}$$

is 36 because the least common multiple of 12 and 18 is 36.

a. The number 0 is even.
b. Lowest common denominator
c. Subtrahend
d. Highest common factor

58. In mathematics, the multiplicative inverse of a number x, denoted 1/x or x^{-1}, is the number which, when multiplied by x, yields 1. The multiplicative inverse of x is also called the _____ of x.
   a. 1-center problem
   b. 120-cell
   c. Reciprocal
   d. 2-3 heap

59. A _____ of a number is a number a such that a^3 = x.
   a. Cube root
   b. Golden function
   c. Hyperbolic functions
   d. Square root

60. In mathematics, an algebraic group G contains a unique maximal normal solvable subgroup; and this subgroup is closed. Its identity component is called the _____ of G.
   a. Block size
   b. Radical
   c. Barycentric coordinates
   d. Composite

61. A _____ is an expression containing a square root.
   a. Controlled Cryptographic Item
   b. Convolution
   c. Convolution theorem
   d. Radical expression

62. In vascular plants, the _____ is the organ of a plant body that typically lies below the surface of the soil. This is not always the case, however, since a _____ can also be aerial (that is, growing above the ground) or aerating (that is, growing up above the ground or especially above water.) Furthermore, a stem normally occurring below ground is not exceptional either
   a. 1-center problem
   b. 120-cell
   c. 2-3 heap
   d. Root

63. In mathematics, a _____ of a number x is a number r such that r^2 = x, or, in other words, a number r whose square is x. Every non-negative real number x has a unique non-negative _____, called the principal _____, which is denoted with a radical symbol as $\sqrt{x}$, or, using exponent notation, as $x^{1/2}$. For example, the principal _____ of 9 is 3, denoted $\sqrt{9}$ = 3, because 3^2 = 3 × 3 = 9.
   a. Multiplicative inverse
   b. Double exponential
   c. Hyperbolic functions
   d. Square root

64. A _____ is the longest side of a right triangle, the side opposite of the right angle. The length of the _____ of a right triangle can be found using the Pythagorean theorem, which states that the square of the length of the _____ equals the sum of the squares of the lengths of the two other sides.

Chapter 1. Basic Concepts of Algebra

For example, if one of the other sides has a length of 3 meters and the other has a length of 4 m.

a. Golden angle
c. Hypotenuse
b. Reflection symmetry
d. Concyclic points

65. In a right triangle, the cathetusoriginally from the Greek word KÎ¬θετος, plural catheti

- 1 Generally
- 2 References
- 3 See also
- 4 External links

In a wider sense, a _____ is any line falling perpendicularly on another line or a surface. Such a line is more commonly known as a surface normal.

a. Line segment
c. Cathetus
b. Face diagonal
d. Central angle

66. In mathematics, the _____ or Pythagoras' theorem is a relation in Euclidean geometry among the three sides of a right triangle. The theorem is named after the Greek mathematician Pythagoras, who by tradition is credited with its discovery and proof, although it is often argued that knowledge of the theory predates him.. The theorem is as follows:

In any right triangle, the area of the square whose side is the hypotenuse is equal to the sum of the areas of the squares whose sides are the two legs.

a. 2-3 heap
c. Pythagorean theorem
b. 120-cell
d. 1-center problem

67. A _____ is one of the basic shapes of geometry: a polygon with three corners or vertices and three sides or edges which are line segments. A _____ with vertices A, B, and C is denoted ABC.

In Euclidean geometry any three non-collinear points determine a unique _____ and a unique plane.

a. 1-center problem
c. Kepler triangle
b. Fuhrmann circle
d. Triangle

68. In mathematics, a _____ is a statement that can be proved on the basis of explicitly stated or previously agreed assumptions.

a. Disjunction introduction
c. Boolean function
b. Logical value
d. Theorem

69. In algebra, a _____ of an element in a quadratic extension field of a field K is its image under the unique non-identity automorphism of the extended field that fixes K. If the extension is generated by a square root of an element r of K, then the _____ of $a + b\sqrt{r}$ is $a - b\sqrt{r}$ for $a, b \in K$, and in particular in the case of the field C of complex numbers as an extension of the field R of real numbers, the complex _____ of a + bi is a − bi.

Forming the sum or product of any element of the extension field with its _____ always gives an element of K.

a. Real structure
b. Trinomial
c. Relation algebra
d. Conjugate

70. In geometry, an _____ is a triangle in which all three sides have equal lengths. In traditional or Euclidean geometry, _____s are also equiangular; that is, all three internal angles are also equal to each other and are each 60°. They are regular polygons, and can therefore also be referred to as regular triangles.

a. Isotomic conjugate
b. A chemical equation
c. A Mathematical Theory of Communication
d. Equilateral triangle

71. _____ is a quantity expressing the two-dimensional size of a defined part of a surface, typically a region bounded by a closed curve. The term surface _____ refers to the total _____ of the exposed surface of a 3-dimensional solid, such as the sum of the _____s of the exposed sides of a polyhedron. _____ is an important invariant in the differential geometry of surfaces.

a. A chemical equation
b. A posteriori
c. Area
d. A Mathematical Theory of Communication

72. A _____ is the transfer of an interest in property (or in law the equivalent - a charge) to a lender as a security for a debt - usually a loan of money. While a _____ in itself is not a debt, it is lender's security for a debt. It is a transfer of an interest in land (or the equivalent), from the owner to the _____ lender, on the condition that this interest will be returned to the owner of the real estate when the terms of the _____ have been satisfied or performed.

a. 2-3 heap
b. Mortgage
c. 1-center problem
d. 120-cell

Chapter 2. Graphs, Functions, and Models

1. A bar chart or _____ is a chart with rectangular bars with lengths proportional to the values that they represent. Bar charts are used for comparing two or more values. The bars can be horizontally or vertically oriented.
   a. 120-cell
   b. 2-3 heap
   c. 1-center problem
   d. Bar graph

2. The x-axis is the horizontal axis of a two- dimensional plot in the _____, that is typically pointed to the right. Also known as a right-handed coordinate system.
   a. Cartesian coordinate system
   b. 120-cell
   c. 2-3 heap
   d. 1-center problem

3. A _____ is a simple shape of Euclidean geometry consisting of those points in a plane which are at a constant distance, called the radius, from a fixed point, called the center. A _____ with center A is sometimes denoted by the symbol A.

   A chord of a _____ is a line segment whose two endpoints lie on the _____.

   a. Malfatti circles
   b. Circumcircle
   c. Circular segment
   d. Circle

4. In graph theory, a _____ is a graph whose vertices can be associated with chords of a circle such that two vertices are adjacent if and only if the corresponding chords in the circle intersect.

   Spinrad (1994) gives an $O(n^2)$-time recognition algorithm for _____s that also computes a circle model of the input graph if it is a _____.

   A number of other problems that are NP-complete on general graphs have polynomial time algorithms when restricted to _____s.

   a. Sparse graph
   b. Vertex-transitive graph
   c. Planar graph
   d. Circle graph

5. In a graph theory, the _____ L

   One of the earliest and most important theorems about _____s is due to Hassler Whitney, who proved that with one exceptional case the structure of G can be recovered completely from its _____.

   a. Vertex-transitive graph
   b. Sparse graph
   c. Bivariegated graph
   d. Line graph

6. In quantum field theory and statistical mechanics in the thermodynamic limit, a system with a global symmetry can have more than one phase. For parameters where the symmetry is spontaneously broken, the system is said to be _____. When the global symmetry is unbroken the system is disordered.
   a. Ursell function
   b. Ordered
   c. Einstein relation
   d. Isoenthalpic-isobaric ensemble

Chapter 2. Graphs, Functions, and Models

7. In mathematics, an _____ is a collection of objects having two coordinates (or entries or projections), such that one can always uniquely determine the object, which is the first coordinate (or first entry or left projection) of the pair as well as the second coordinate (or second entry or right projection.) If the first coordinate is a and the second is b, the usual notation for an _____ is (a, b.) The pair is 'ordered' in that (a, b) differs from (b, a) unless a = b.
   - a. A Mathematical Theory of Communication
   - b. A chemical equation
   - c. Ordered pair
   - d. A posteriori

8. In mathematics, the _____ of a Euclidean space is a special point, usually denoted by the letter O, used as a fixed point of reference for the geometry of the surrounding space. In a Cartesian coordinate system, the _____ is the point where the axes of the system intersect. In Euclidean geometry, the _____ may be chosen freely as any convenient point of reference.
   - a. Origin
   - b. Autonomous system
   - c. Interval
   - d. OMAC

9. A _____ consists of one quarter of the coordinate plane.
   - a. 1-center problem
   - b. 120-cell
   - c. 2-3 heap
   - d. Quadrant

10. A _____ is an opening in a wall that allows the passage of light and, if not closed or sealed, air and sound. _____s are usually glazed or covered in some other transparent or translucent material. _____s are held in place by frames, which prevent them from collapsing in.
    - a. 120-cell
    - b. 2-3 heap
    - c. 1-center problem
    - d. Window

11. An _____ of a real-valued function y = f(x) is a curve which describes the behavior of f as either x or y tends to infinity.

    In other words, as one moves along the graph of f(x) in some direction, the distance between it and the _____ eventually becomes smaller than any distance that one may specify.

    If a curve A has the curve B as an _____, one says that A is asymptotic to B. Similarly B is asymptotic to A, so A and B are called asymptotic.

    - a. Improper integral
    - b. Infinite product
    - c. Isoperimetric dimension
    - d. Asymptote

12. The _____ is the horizontal axis of a two- dimensional plot in the Cartesian coordinate system, that is typically pointed to the right. Also known as a right-handed coordinate system.
    - a. X-axis
    - b. 120-cell
    - c. 2-3 heap
    - d. 1-center problem

13. In reference to a 2D and 3D plane, the _____ is the vertical height of a 2D or 3D object.
    - a. 1-center problem
    - b. 120-cell
    - c. 2-3 heap
    - d. Y-axis

Chapter 2. Graphs, Functions, and Models

14. The term _____ or centre is used in various contexts in abstract algebra to denote the set of all those elements that commute with all other elements. More specifically:

- The _____ of a group G consists of all those elements x in G such that xg = gx for all g in G. This is a normal subgroup of G.
- The _____ of a ring R is the subset of R consisting of all those elements x of R such that xr = rx for all r in R. The _____ is a commutative subring of R, so R is an algebra over its _____.
- The _____ of an algebra A consists of all those elements x of A such that xa = ax for all a in A. See also: central simple algebra.
- The _____ of a Lie algebra L consists of all those elements x in L such that [x,a] = 0 for all a in L. This is an ideal of the Lie algebra L.
- The _____ of a monoidal category C consists of pairs *a natural isomorphism satisfying certain axioms*.

a. Center
b. Brute Force
c. Block size
d. Disk

15. In mathematics an _____ , a 'falling short') is a conic section, the locus of points in a plane such that the sum of the distances to two fixed points is equal to a given constant. The two fixed points are then called foci.

Another way is to define it as the path traced out by a point whose distance from a focus maintains a constant ratio less than one with its distance from a straight line not passing through the focus, called the directrix.

a. A Mathematical Theory of Communication
b. A posteriori
c. A chemical equation
d. Ellipse

16. The _____ is one of the coordinates of a point in a two or three-dimensional cartesian coordinate system, equal to the distance of a point from the y-axis in a 2D system, or from the plane of y and z axes in a 3D system, measured along a line parallel to the x axis.

a. 120-cell
b. 1-center problem
c. 2-3 heap
d. X-coordinate

17. The _____ is the distance between a point and an axis in the Cartesian Coordinate System.

a. 2-3 heap
b. 1-center problem
c. 120-cell
d. Y-coordinate

18. In mathematics, the _____ is an approach to finding a particular solution to certain inhomogeneous ordinary differential equations and recurrence relations. It is closely related to the annihilator method, but instead of using a particular kind of differential operator in order to find the best possible form of the particular solution, a 'guess' is made as to the appropriate form, which is then tested by differentiating the resulting equation. In this sense, the _____ is less formal but more intuitive than the annihilator method.

a. Differential algebraic equations
b. Phase line
c. Linear differential equation
d. Method of undetermined coefficients

Chapter 2. Graphs, Functions, and Models

19. In geometry and trigonometry, an _____ is the figure formed by two rays sharing a common endpoint, called the vertex of the _____. The magnitude of the _____ is the 'amount of rotation' that separates the two rays, and can be measured by considering the length of circular arc swept out when one ray is rotated about the vertex to coincide with the other. Where there is no possibility of confusion, the term '_____' is used interchangeably for both the geometric configuration itself and for its angular magnitude.

   a. A posteriori
   b. A chemical equation
   c. A Mathematical Theory of Communication
   d. Angle

20. In mathematics, a _____ on a fiber bundle is a device that defines a notion of parallel transport on the bundle; that is, a way to 'connect' or identify fibers over nearby points. If the fiber bundle is a vector bundle, then the notion of parallel transport is required to be linear. Such a _____ is equivalently specified by a covariant derivative, which is an operator that can differentiate sections of that bundle along tangent directions in the base manifold.

   a. 120-cell
   b. Connection
   c. Connectivity
   d. 1-center problem

21. _____ and independent variables refer to values that change in relationship to each other. The _____ are those that are observed to change in response to the independent variables. The independent variables are those that are deliberately manipulated to invoke a change in the _____.

   a. Steiner system
   b. Dependent variables
   c. Yates analysis
   d. Round robin test

22. Dependent variables and _____ refer to values that change in relationship to each other. The dependent variables are those that are observed to change in response to the _____. The _____ are those that are deliberately manipulated to invoke a change in the dependent variables.

   a. Independent variables
   b. One-factor-at-a-time method
   c. Experimental design diagram
   d. Operational confound

23. In geometry, a _____ is a special kind of point, usually a corner of a polygon, polyhedron, or higher dimensional polytope. In the geometry of curves a _____ is a point of where the first derivative of curvature is zero. In graph theory, a _____ is the fundamental unit out of which graphs are formed

   a. Crib
   b. Dini
   c. Duality
   d. Vertex

24. In statistics, the _____ is the value that occurs the most frequently in a data set or a probability distribution. In some fields, notably education, sample data are often called scores, and the sample _____ is known as the modal score.

   Like the statistical mean and the median, the _____ is a way of capturing important information about a random variable or a population in a single quantity.

   a. Field
   b. Function
   c. Deltoid
   d. Mode

25. In mathematics and in the sciences, a _____ (plural: _____e, formulæ or _____s) is a concise way of expressing information symbolically (as in a mathematical or chemical _____), or a general relationship between quantities. One of many famous _____e is Albert Einstein's $E = mc^2$ (see special relativity

Chapter 2. Graphs, Functions, and Models

In mathematics, a _____ is a key to solve an equation with variables. For example, the problem of determining the volume of a sphere is one that requires a significant amount of integral calculus to solve.

a. 1-center problem
c. 2-3 heap
b. 120-cell
d. Formula

26. In classical geometry, a _____ of a circle or sphere is any line segment from its center to its boundary. By extension, the _____ of a circle or sphere is the length of any such segment. The _____ is half the diameter. In science and engineering the term _____ of curvature is commonly used as a synonym for _____.

a. Birational geometry
c. Duoprism
b. Non-Euclidean geometry
d. Radius

27. _____ is an algebraic technique used to solve quadratic equations, in analytic geometry for determining the shapes of graphs, and in calculus for computing integrals. The essential objective is to reduce a quadratic polynomial in a variable in an equation or expression to a squared polynomial of linear order. This can reduce an equation or integral to one that is more easily solved or evaluated.

a. Monomial basis
c. Relation algebra
b. Permanent of a matrix
d. Completing the square

28. A _____ typically refers to a class of handheld calculators that are capable of plotting graphs, solving simultaneous equations, and performing numerous other tasks with variables. Most popular _____s are also programmable, allowing the user to create customized programs, typically for scientific/engineering and education applications. Due to their large displays intended for graphing, they can also accommodate several lines of text and calculations at a time.

a. Bump mapping
c. Genus
b. Support vector machines
d. Graphing calculator

29. In mathematics, the _____ of a real number is its numerical value without regard to its sign. So, for example, 3 is the _____ of both 3 and −3.

The _____ of a number a is denoted by $|a|$.

Generalizations of the _____ for real numbers occur in a wide variety of mathematical settings.

a. Area hyperbolic functions
c. Absolute value
b. A Mathematical Theory of Communication
d. A chemical equation

30. A _____ is a device for performing mathematical calculations, distinguished from a computer by having a limited problem solving ability and an interface optimized for interactive calculation rather than programming. _____s can be hardware or software, and mechanical or electronic, and are often built into devices such as PDAs or mobile phones.

Modern electronic _____s are generally small, digital, and usually inexpensive.

a. 120-cell
b. 1-center problem
c. 2-3 heap
d. Calculator

31. In mathematics, the _____ or Pythagoras' theorem is a relation in Euclidean geometry among the three sides of a right triangle. The theorem is named after the Greek mathematician Pythagoras, who by tradition is credited with its discovery and proof, although it is often argued that knowledge of the theory predates him.. The theorem is as follows:

In any right triangle, the area of the square whose side is the hypotenuse is equal to the sum of the areas of the squares whose sides are the two legs.

a. 120-cell
b. 2-3 heap
c. 1-center problem
d. Pythagorean theorem

32. In mathematics, a _____ is a statement that can be proved on the basis of explicitly stated or previously agreed assumptions.
a. Boolean function
b. Disjunction introduction
c. Logical value
d. Theorem

33. In mathematics, a _____ is a circle with a unit radius. Frequently, especially in trigonometry, 'the' _____ is the circle of radius 1 centered at the origin in the Cartesian coordinate system in the Euclidean plane. The _____ is often denoted S^1; the generalization to higher dimensions is the unit sphere.
a. Inscribed angle theorem
b. Open unit disk
c. Excircle
d. Unit circle

34. In mathematics, especially in the area of abstract algebra known as ring theory, a _____ is a ring with 0 ≠ 1 such that ab = 0 implies that either a = 0 or b = 0. That is, it is a nontrivial ring without left or right zero divisors. A commutative _____ is called an integral _____.
a. Left primitive ring
b. Domain
c. Modular representation theory
d. Simple ring

35. In mathematics, an _____ or member of a set is any one of the distinct objects that make up that set.

Writing A = {1,2,3,4}, means that the _____s of the set A are the numbers 1, 2, 3 and 4. Groups of _____s of A, for example {1,2}, are subsets of A.

a. Universal code
b. Ideal
c. Order
d. Element

36. The mathematical concept of a _____ expresses the intuitive idea of deterministic dependence between two quantities, one of which is viewed as primary and the other as secondary. A _____ then is a way to associate a unique output for each input of a specified type, for example, a real number or an element of a given set.
a. Grill
b. Coherent
c. Going up
d. Function

37. In descriptive statistics, the _____ is the length of the smallest interval which contains all the data. It is calculated by subtracting the smallest observations from the greatest and provides an indication of statistical dispersion.

It is measured in the same units as the data.

a. Kernel
b. Bandwidth
c. Range
d. Class

38. In elementary algebra, a _____ is a polynomial with two terms: the sum of two monomials. It is the simplest kind of polynomial except for a monomial.

The _____ $a^2 - b^2$ can be factored as the product of two other _____s:

$a^2 - b^2$.

The product of a pair of linear _____s a x + b and c x + d is:

2 +x + bd.

A _____ raised to the nth power, represented as

n

can be expanded by means of the _____ theorem or, equivalently, using Pascal's triangle.

a. Cylindrical algebraic decomposition
b. Real structure
c. Rational root theorem
d. Binomial

39. In mathematics, the _____ $\binom{n}{k}$ is the coefficient of the x^k term in the polynomial expansion of the binomial power ^{n}.

In combinatorics, $\binom{n}{k}$ is interpreted as the number of k-element subsets of an n-element set, that is the number of ways that k things can be 'chosen' from a set of n things. Hence, $\binom{n}{k}$ is often read as 'n choose k' and called the choose function of n and k.

a. Symbolic combinatorics
b. Rule of product
c. Dyson conjecture
d. Binomial coefficient

40. In mathematics, a _____ is a constant multiplicative factor of a certain object. For example, in the expression $9x^2$, the _____ of x^2 is 9.

The object can be such things as a variable, a vector, a function, etc.

a. Stability radius
c. Coefficient
b. Fibonacci polynomials
d. Multivariate division algorithm

41. To define the derivative of a distribution, we first consider the case of a differentiable and integrable function f : R → R. If φ is a _____, then we have

$$\int_R f'\varphi\, dx = -\int_R f\varphi'\, dx$$

using integration by parts (note that φ is zero outside of a bounded set and that therefore no boundary values have to be taken into account.) This suggests that if S is a distribution, we should define its derivative S' by

$$\langle S', \varphi \rangle = -\langle S, \varphi' \rangle.$$

a. Generalized functions
c. Hyperfunction
b. Schwartz kernel theorem
d. Test Function

42. In set theory, the term _____ refers to a set operation used in the convergence of set elements to form a resultant set containing the elements of both sets. As a simple example, a _____ of two disjoint sets, which do not have elements in common results in a set containing all elements from both sets. A Venn diagram representing the _____ of sets A and B.

a. UES
c. Event
b. Union
d. Introduction

43. A _____ is a software program that facilitates symbolic mathematics. The core functionality of a CAS is manipulation of mathematical expressions in symbolic form.

Chapter 2. Graphs, Functions, and Models 25

The symbolic manipulations supported typically include

- simplification to the smallest possible expression or some standard form, including automatic simplification with assumptions and simplification with constraints
- substitution of symbolic, functors or numeric values for expressions
- change of form of expressions: expanding products and powers, partial and full factorization, rewriting as partial fractions, constraint satisfaction, rewriting trigonometric functions as exponentials, etc.
- partial and total differentiation
- symbolic constrained and unconstrained global optimization
- solution of linear and some non-linear equations over various domains
- solution of some differential and difference equations
- taking some limits
- some indefinite and definite integration, including multidimensional integrals
- integral transforms
- arbitrary-precision numeric operations
- Series operations such as expansion, summation and products
- matrix operations including products, inverses, etc.
- display of mathematical expressions in two-dimensional mathematical form, often using typesetting systems similar to TeX
- add-ons for use in applied mathematics such as physics packages for physical computation
- plotting graphs and parametric plots of functions in two and three dimensions, and animating them
- APIs for linking it on an external program such as a database, or using in a programming language to use the _____
- drawing charts and diagrams
- string manipulation such as matching and searching
- statistical computation
- Theorem proving and verification
- graphic production and editing such as CGI and signal processing as image processing
- sound synthesis

Many also include a programming language, allowing users to implement their own algorithms.

Some _____ s focus on a specific area of application; these are typically developed in academia and are free.

a. Computer algebra system   b. 2-3 heap
c. 1-center problem   d. 120-cell

44. The Q-TIP of a geographic location is its height above a fixed reference point, often the mean sea level. _____, or geometric height, is mainly used when referring to points on the Earth's surface, while altitude or geopotential height is used for points above the surface, such as an aircraft in flight or a spacecraft in orbit.

Less commonly, _____ is measured using the center of the Earth as the reference point.

a. A Mathematical Theory of Communication
b. A chemical equation
c. A posteriori
d. Elevation

45. _____ is a quantity expressing the two-dimensional size of a defined part of a surface, typically a region bounded by a closed curve. The term surface _____ refers to the total _____ of the exposed surface of a 3-dimensional solid, such as the sum of the _____s of the exposed sides of a polyhedron. _____ is an important invariant in the differential geometry of surfaces.
   a. A Mathematical Theory of Communication
   b. A chemical equation
   c. A posteriori
   d. Area

46. A _____ is an abstract model that uses mathematical language to describe the behavior of a system. Eykhoff defined a _____ as 'a representation of the essential aspects of an existing system which presents knowledge of that system in usable form'.
   a. Rata Die
   b. Mathematical model
   c. Total least squares
   d. Metaheuristic

47. In ecology, predation describes a biological interaction where a _____ (an organism that is hunting) feeds on its prey, the organism that is attacked. _____s may or may not kill their prey prior to feeding on them, but the act of predation always results in the death of the prey. The other main category of consumption is detritivory, the consumption of dead organic material (detritus.)
   a. 1-center problem
   b. 120-cell
   c. Prey
   d. Predator

48. In mathematics, a _____ is a system which is not linear. Less technically, a _____ is any problem where the variabl to be solved for cannot be written as a linear sum of independent components. A nonhomogenous system, which is linear apart from the presence of a function of the independent variables, is nonlinear according to a strict definition, but such systems are usually studied alongside linear systems, because they can be transformed to a linear system as long as a particular solution is known.
   a. George Dantzig
   b. 1-center problem
   c. Nonlinear system
   d. Metric system

49. In mathematics, a _____ of a set X is a collection of sets such that X is a subset of the union of sets in the collection. In symbols, if

$$C = \{U_\alpha : \alpha \in A\}$$

is an indexed family of sets U_α, then C is a _____ of X if

$$X \subseteq \bigcup_{\alpha \in A} U_\alpha$$

_____s are commonly used in the context of topology. If the set X is a topological space, then a _____ C of X is a collection of subsets U_α of X whose union is the whole space X.

a. Cover
c. Manifold
b. Generalised metric
d. Contractible space

50. In mathematics, a _____ is a function whose values do not vary and thus are constant. For example, if we have the function f→ B is a _____ if f
    a. Linear operator
    c. Squeeze mapping
    b. Point reflection
    d. Constant function

51. In mathematics, the term _____ has several different important meanings:

- An _____ is an equality that remains true regardless of the values of any variables that appear within it, to distinguish it from an equality which is true under more particular conditions. For this, the 'triple bar' symbol ≡ is sometimes used.
- In algebra, an _____ or _____ element of a set S with a binary operation Â· is an element e that, when combined with any element x of S, produces that same x. That is, eÂ·x = xÂ·e = x for all x in S.
    - The _____ function from a set S to itself, often denoted id or id$_S$, s the function such that i = x for all x in S. This function serves as the _____ element in the set of all functions from S to itself with respect to function composition.
    - In linear algebra, the _____ matrix of size n is the n-by-n square matrix with ones on the main diagonal and zeros elsewhere. This matrix serves as the _____ with respect to matrix multiplication.

A common example of the first meaning is the trigonometric _____

$$\sin^2 \theta + \cos^2 \theta = 1$$

which is true for all real values of θ, as opposed to

$$\cos \theta = 1,$$

which is true only for some values of θ, not all. For example, the latter equation is true when $\theta = 0$, false when $\theta = 2$

The concepts of 'additive _____' and 'multiplicative _____' are central to the Peano axioms. The number 0 is the 'additive _____' for integers, real numbers, and complex numbers. For the real numbers, for all $a \in \mathbb{R}$,

$$0 + a = a,$$

$a + 0 = a,$ and

$$0 + 0 = 0.$$

Similarly, The number 1 is the 'multiplicative _____' for integers, real numbers, and complex numbers.

a. Action
b. Intersection
c. ARIA
d. Identity

52. An _____ is a function that does not have any effect: it always returns the same value that was used as its argument.
   a. Angle bisector
   b. Inverse function
   c. Algebra
   d. Identity function

53. _____ is used to describe the steepness, incline, gradient, or grade of a straight line. A higher _____ value indicates a steeper incline. The _____ is defined as the ratio of the 'rise' divided by the 'run' between two points on a line, or in other words, the ratio of the altitude change to the horizontal distance between any two points on the line.
   a. Point plotting
   b. Number line
   c. Cognitively Guided Instruction
   d. Slope

54. In mathematics, an _____, or central tendency of a data set refers to a measure of the 'middle' or 'expected' value of the data set. There are many different descriptive statistics that can be chosen as a measurement of the central tendency of the data items.

An _____ is a single value that is meant to typify a list of values.

   a. A chemical equation
   b. Average
   c. A Mathematical Theory of Communication
   d. A posteriori

55. _____ is the measurement of vertical distance, but has two meanings in common use. It can either indicate how 'tall' something is, or how 'high up' it is. For example one could say 'That is a tall building', or 'That airplane is high up in the sky'.
   a. Height
   b. 120-cell
   c. 2-3 heap
   d. 1-center problem

56. In the physical sciences, _____ is a measurement of the gravitational force acting on an object. Near the surface of the Earth, the acceleration due to gravity is approximately constant; this means that an object's _____ is roughly proportional to its mass.

In commerce and in many other applications, _____ means the same as mass as that term is used in physics.

   a. 120-cell
   b. 1-center problem
   c. 2-3 heap
   d. Weight

57. In commutative and homological algebra, _____ is an important invariant of rings and modules. Although _____ can be defined more generally, the most common case considered is the case of modules over a commutative Noetherian local ring. In this case, the _____ of a module is related with its projective dimension by the Auslander-Buchsbaum formula.
   a. Basis
   b. Closeness
   c. Closed form
   d. Depth

Chapter 2. Graphs, Functions, and Models

58. In ring theory, a branch of abstract algebra, an _____ is a special subset of a ring. The _____ concept generalizes in an appropriate way some important properties of integers like 'even number' or 'multiple of 3'.

For instance, in rings one studies prime _____s instead of prime numbers, one defines coprime _____s as a generalization of coprime numbers, and one can prove a generalized Chinese remainder theorem about _____s.

- a. Ideal
- b. Equity
- c. Equaliser
- d. Element

59. In computational complexity theory, an algorithm is said to take _____ if the asymptotic upper bound for the time it requires is proportional to the size of the input, which is usually denoted n.

Informally spoken, the running time increases linearly with the size of the input. For example, a procedure that adds up all elements of a list requires time proportional to the length of the list.

- a. Time-constructible function
- b. Constructible function
- c. Truth table reduction
- d. Linear time

60. In economics, business, retail, and accounting, a _____ is the value of money that has been used up to produce something, and hence is not available for use anymore. In business, the _____ may be one of acquisition, in which case the amount of money expended to acquire it is counted as _____. In this case, money is the input that is gone in order to acquire the thing.

- a. 120-cell
- b. 1-center problem
- c. 2-3 heap
- d. Cost

61. _____ is a term used in accounting, economics and finance to spread the cost of an asset over the span of several years.

In simple words we can say that _____ is the reduction in the value of an asset due to usage, passage of time, wear and tear, technological outdating or obsolescence, depletion or other such factors.

In accounting, _____ is a term used to describe any method of attributing the historical or purchase cost of an asset across its useful life, roughly corresponding to normal wear and tear.

- a. Gross sales
- b. Depreciation
- c. 1-center problem
- d. 120-cell

62. A _____ is an algebraic equation in which each term is either a constant or the product of a constant and a single variable. _____s can have one, two, three or more variables.

_____s occur with great regularity in applied mathematics.

Chapter 2. Graphs, Functions, and Models

a. Linear equation
b. Quadratic equation
c. Quartic equation
d. Difference of two squares

63. A _____ of a curve is the envelope of a family of congruent circles centered on the curve. It generalises the concept of _____ lines.

It is sometimes called the offset curve but the term 'offset' often refers also to translation.

a. Bifolium
b. Cissoid
c. Cycloid
d. Parallel

64. The existence and properties of _____ are the basis of Euclid's parallel postulate. _____ are two lines on the same plane that do not intersect even assuming that lines extend to infinity in either direction.

a. Spidron
b. Parallel lines
c. Vertical translation
d. Square wheel

65. In mathematics, the concept of a _____ tries to capture the intuitive idea of a geometrical one-dimensional and continuous object. A simple example is the circle. In everyday use of the term '_____', a straight line is not curved, but in mathematical parlance _____s include straight lines and line segments.

a. Quadrifolium
b. Negative pedal curve
c. Kappa curve
d. Curve

66. _____ is finding a curve which has the best fit to a series of data points and possibly other constraints. This section is an introduction to both interpolation and regression analysis. Both are sometimes used for extrapolation.

a. Curve fitting
b. Numerical stability
c. Multiphysics
d. Spectral methods

67. In probability theory and statistics, _____ indicates the strength and direction of a linear relationship between two random variables. That is in contrast with the usage of the term in colloquial speech, denoting any relationship, not necessarily linear. In general statistical usage, _____ or co-relation refers to the departure of two random variables from independence.

a. Summary statistics
b. Correlation
c. Sample size
d. Random variables

68. In statistics, _____ is a form of regression analysis in which the relationship between one or more independent variables and another variable, called dependent variable, is modeled by a least squares function, called _____ equation. This function is a linear combination of one or more model parameters, called regression coefficients. A _____ equation with one independent variable represents a straight line.

a. Percentile rank
b. Kurtosis
c. Random variables
d. Linear regression

69. The _____ is a unit of plane angle, equal to 180/π degrees, or about 57.2958 degrees. It is the standard unit of angular measurement in all areas of mathematics beyond the elementary level.

The _____ is represented by the symbol 'rad' or, more rarely, by the superscript c.

Chapter 2. Graphs, Functions, and Models

    a. 120-cell   b. RADIAN
    c. 1-center problem   d. 2-3 heap

70. The _____ fallacy is an informal fallacy. It ascribes cause where none exists. The flaw is failing to account for natural fluctuations.
    a. Depth   b. Differential
    c. Degrees of freedom   d. Regression

71. In calculus, a function f defined on a subset of the real numbers with real values is called monotonic (also monotonically increasing or non-_____), if for all x and y such that x ≤ y one has f(x) ≤ f(y), so f preserves the order. In layman's terms, the sign of the slope is always positive (the curve tending upwards) or zero (i.e., non-_____, or asymptotic, or depicted as a horizontal, flat line) Likewise, a function is called monotonically _____ (non-increasing) if, whenever x ≤ y, then f(x) ≥ f(y), so it reverses the order.
    a. Dual pair   b. Tensor product of Hilbert spaces
    c. Circular convolution   d. Decreasing

72. In mathematics, _____ is a technique for optimization of a linear objective function, subject to linear equality and linear inequality constraints. Informally, _____ determines the way to achieve the best outcome in a given mathematical model given some list of requirements represented as linear equations.

More formally, given a polytope, and a real-valued affine function

$$f(x_1, x_2, \ldots, x_n) = c_1 x_1 + c_2 x_2 + \cdots + c_n x_n + d$$

defined on this polytope, a _____ method will find a point in the polytope where this function has the smallest value.

    a. Linear programming   b. Linear programming relaxation
    c. Descent direction   d. Lin-Kernighan

73. In mathematics, _____ and minima, known collectively as extrema, are the largest value or smallest value, that a function takes in a point either within a given neighbourhood or on the function domain in its entirety.

A real-valued function f' defined on the real line is said to have a local maximum point at the point x*, if there exists some ε > 0, such that f≥ f½x − x*| < ε. The value of the function at this point is called maximum of the function.

    a. Field   b. Descent
    c. Decimal system   d. Maxima

74. _____ are points in the domain of a function at which the function takes a largest value or smallest value, either within a given neighborhood or on the function domain in its entirety.
    a. Test for Divergence   b. Calculus controversy
    c. Minima   d. Maxima and minima

75. In mathematics, maxima and _____, known collectively as extrema, are the largest value or smallest value, that a function takes in a point either within a given neighbourhood or on the function domain in its entirety.

A real-valued function f' defined on the real line is said to have a local maximum point at the point x*, if there exists some ε > 0, such that f≥ f½x − x* | < ε. The value of the function at this point is called maximum of the function.

a. Periodic function
c. Calculus
b. Dirichlet integral
d. Minima

76. In mathematics, a _____ is a function whose definition is dependent on the value of the independent variable. Mathematically, a real-valued function f of a real variable x is a relationship whose definition is given differently on disjoint subsets of its domain

The word piecewise is also used to describe any property of a _____ that holds for each piece but may not hold for the whole domain of the function.

a. Glide reflection
c. Piecewise-defined function
b. Surjective
d. High-dimensional model representation

77. In mathematics, _____ and undefined are used to explain whether or not expressions have meaningful, sensible, and unambiguous values. Not all branches of mathematics come to the same conclusion.

The following expressions are undefined in all contexts, but remarks in the analysis section may apply.

a. LHS
c. Toy model
b. Plugging in
d. Defined

78. The _____ are the set of numbers consisting of the natural numbers including 0 and their negatives. They are numbers that can be written without a fractional or decimal component, and fall within the set {... −2, −1, 0, 1, 2, ...}.

a. A chemical equation
c. A posteriori
b. Integers
d. A Mathematical Theory of Communication

79. _____ is the mathematical operation of scaling one number by another. It is one of the four basic operations in elementary arithmetic.

_____ is defined for whole numbers in terms of repeated addition; for example, 4 multiplied by 3 can be calculated by adding 3 copies of 4 together:

$$4 + 4 + 4 = 12.$$

_____ of rational numbers and real numbers is defined by systematic generalization of this basic idea.

Chapter 2. Graphs, Functions, and Models

a. Multiplication
c. Highest common factor
b. Least common multiple
d. The number 0 is even.

80. In mathematics, a _____ is the end result of a division problem. It can also be expressed as the number of times the divisor divides into the dividend.
   a. Marginal cost
   c. Notation
   b. Limiting
   d. Quotient

81. In mathematics, an arithmetic progression or _____ is a sequence of numbers such that the difference of any two successive members of the sequence is a constant. For instance, the sequence 3, 5, 7, 9, 11, 13... is an arithmetic progression with common difference 2.
   a. Eisenstein series
   c. Edgeworth series
   b. Alternating series test
   d. Arithmetic sequence

82. In mathematics, _____ is a property that a binary operation can have. It means that, within an expression containing two or more of the same associative operators in a row, the order that the operations are performed does not matter as long as the sequence of the operands is not changed. That is, rearranging the parentheses in such an expression will not change its value.
   a. Unital
   c. Algebraically closed
   b. Idempotence
   d. Associativity

83. In mathematics, the _____s are an extension of the real numbers obtained by adjoining an imaginary unit, denoted i, which satisfies:

$$i^2 = -1.$$

Every _____ can be written in the form a + bi, where a and b are real numbers called the real part and the imaginary part of the _____, respectively.

_____s are a field, and thus have addition, subtraction, multiplication, and division operations. These operations extend the corresponding operations on real numbers, although with a number of additional elegant and useful properties, e.g., negative real numbers can be obtained by squaring _____s.

   a. Real part
   c. 120-cell
   b. Complex number
   d. 1-center problem

84. A _____ number is a positive integer which has a positive divisor other than one or itself. By definition, every integer greater than one is either a prime number or a _____ number.zero and one are considered to be neither prime nor _____. For example, the integer 14 is a _____ number because it can be factored as 2 × 7.
   a. Discontinuity
   c. Composite
   b. Basis
   d. Key server

34 Chapter 2. Graphs, Functions, and Models

85. _____ is a term in mathematics. It can refer to:

- a _____ line, in geometry
- the trigonometric function called _____
- the _____ method, a root-finding algorithm in numerical analysis

a. Large set
c. Separable
b. Solvable
d. Secant

86. _____ generally conveys two primary meanings. The first is an imprecise sense of harmonious or aesthetically-pleasing proportionality and balance; such that it reflects beauty or perfection. The second meaning is a precise and well-defined concept of balance or 'patterned self-similarity' that can be demonstrated or proved according to the rules of a formal system: by geometry, through physics or otherwise.
   a. Tessellation
   c. Symmetry breaking
   b. Molecular symmetry
   d. Symmetry

87. In mathematics, even functions and _____s are functions which satisfy particular symmetry relations, with respect to taking additive inverses. They are important in many areas of mathematical analysis, especially the theory of power series and Fourier series. They are named for the parity of the powers of the power functions which satisfy each condition: the function f(x) = x^n is an even function if n is an even integer, and it is an _____ if n is an odd integer.
   a. A Mathematical Theory of Communication
   c. A posteriori
   b. A chemical equation
   d. Odd function

88. In mathematics, a _____ of a number x is a number r such that r^2 = x, or, in other words, a number r whose square is x. Every non-negative real number x has a unique non-negative _____, called the principal _____, which is denoted with a radical symbol as $\sqrt{x}$, or, using exponent notation, as $x^{1/2}$. For example, the principal _____ of 9 is 3, denoted $\sqrt{9}$ = 3, because 3^2 = 3 × 3 = 9.
   a. Multiplicative inverse
   c. Double exponential
   b. Hyperbolic functions
   d. Square root

89. In vascular plants, the _____ is the organ of a plant body that typically lies below the surface of the soil. This is not always the case, however, since a _____ can also be aerial (that is, growing above the ground) or aerating (that is, growing up above the ground or especially above water.) Furthermore, a stem normally occurring below ground is not exceptional either
   a. 120-cell
   c. 1-center problem
   b. 2-3 heap
   d. Root

90. A _____ of a number is a number a such that a^3 = x.
   a. Hyperbolic functions
   c. Golden function
   b. Cube root
   d. Square root

91. In mathematics, the multiplicative inverse of a number x, denoted 1/x or x^{-1}, is the number which, when multiplied by x, yields 1. The multiplicative inverse of x is also called the _____ of x.

a. 1-center problem
c. 2-3 heap
b. Reciprocal
d. 120-cell

92. _____ is the interpreting of the meaning of a text and the subsequent production of an equivalent text, likewise called a '_____,' that communicates the same message in another language. The text to be translated is called the 'source text,' and the language that it is to be translated into is called the 'target language'; the final product is sometimes called the 'target text.'

_____ must take into account constraints that include context, the rules of grammar of the two languages, their writing conventions, and their idioms. A common misconception is that there exists a simple word-for-word correspondence between any two languages, and that _____ is a straightforward mechanical process; such a word-for-word _____, however, cannot take into account context, grammar, conventions, and idioms.

a. Translation
c. 2-3 heap
b. 120-cell
d. 1-center problem

93. In function graphing, a _____ is a related graph which, for every point (x, y); has a y value which differs from another graph, by exactly some constant c. For example, the antiderivatives of a family are _____s of each other.
   a. Complementary angles
   c. Vertical translation
   b. Parallel postulate
   d. Central angle

Chapter 3. Functions, Equations, and Inequalities

1. In the study of metric spaces in mathematics, there are various notions of two metrics on the same underlying space being 'the same', or _____.

In the following, M will denote a non-empty set and d_1 and d_2 will denote two metrics on M.

The two metrics d_1 and d_2 are said to be topologically _____ if they generate the same topology on M.

   a. A posteriori   b. A Mathematical Theory of Communication
   c. A chemical equation   d. Equivalent

2. A _____ is an algebraic equation in which each term is either a constant or the product of a constant and a single variable. _____s can have one, two, three or more variables.

_____s occur with great regularity in applied mathematics.

   a. Quadratic equation   b. Quartic equation
   c. Difference of two squares   d. Linear equation

3. _____ is the mathematical operation of scaling one number by another. It is one of the four basic operations in elementary arithmetic.

_____ is defined for whole numbers in terms of repeated addition; for example, 4 multiplied by 3 can be calculated by adding 3 copies of 4 together:

$$4 + 4 + 4 = 12.$$

_____ of rational numbers and real numbers is defined by systematic generalization of this basic idea.

   a. Least common multiple   b. The number 0 is even.
   c. Highest common factor   d. Multiplication

4. In mathematics, a _____ on a fiber bundle is a device that defines a notion of parallel transport on the bundle; that is, a way to 'connect' or identify fibers over nearby points. If the fiber bundle is a vector bundle, then the notion of parallel transport is required to be linear. Such a _____ is equivalently specified by a covariant derivative, which is an operator that can differentiate sections of that bundle along tangent directions in the base manifold.
   a. Connectivity   b. 1-center problem
   c. Connection   d. 120-cell

5. The _____ is a unit of plane angle, equal to $180/\pi$ degrees, or about 57.2958 degrees. It is the standard unit of angular measurement in all areas of mathematics beyond the elementary level.

The _____ is represented by the symbol 'rad' or, more rarely, by the superscript c.

   a. RADIAN   b. 120-cell
   c. 1-center problem   d. 2-3 heap

Chapter 3. Functions, Equations, and Inequalities

6. In statistics, the _____ is the value that occurs the most frequently in a data set or a probability distribution. In some fields, notably education, sample data are often called scores, and the sample _____ is known as the modal score.

Like the statistical mean and the median, the _____ is a way of capturing important information about a random variable or a population in a single quantity.

- a. Field
- b. Deltoid
- c. Mode
- d. Function

7. In mathematics and in the sciences, a _____ (plural: _____e, formulæ or _____s) is a concise way of expressing information symbolically (as in a mathematical or chemical _____), or a general relationship between quantities. One of many famous _____e is Albert Einstein's $E = mc^2$ (see special relativity

In mathematics, a _____ is a key to solve an equation with variables. For example, the problem of determining the volume of a sphere is one that requires a significant amount of integral calculus to solve.

- a. 2-3 heap
- b. 120-cell
- c. 1-center problem
- d. Formula

8. _____ is a fee, paid on borrowed capital. Assets lent include money, shares, consumer goods through hire purchase, major assets such as aircraft, and even entire factories in finance lease arrangements. The _____ is calculated upon the value of the assets in the same manner as upon money.

- a. A Mathematical Theory of Communication
- b. Interest sensitivity gap
- c. Interest expense
- d. Interest

9. In abstract algebra, a module S over a ring R is called _____ or irreducible if it is not the zero module 0 and if its only submodules are 0 and S. Understanding the _____ modules over a ring is usually helpful because these modules form the 'building blocks' of all other modules in a certain sense.

Abelian groups are the same as Z-modules.

- a. Harmonic series
- b. Basis
- c. Derivation
- d. Simple

10. The _____ is the length of the line that bounds an area In the special case where the area is circular, the _____ is known as the circumference.
- a. Concyclic
- b. Perimeter
- c. Multilateration
- d. Reflection symmetry

11. The mathematical concept of a _____ expresses the intuitive idea of deterministic dependence between two quantities, one of which is viewed as primary and the other as secondary. A _____ then is a way to associate a unique output for each input of a specified type, for example, a real number or an element of a given set.
- a. Going up
- b. Coherent
- c. Function
- d. Grill

Chapter 3. Functions, Equations, and Inequalities

12. A _____ is an opening in a wall that allows the passage of light and, if not closed or sealed, air and sound. _____s are usually glazed or covered in some other transparent or translucent material. _____s are held in place by frames, which prevent them from collapsing in.

   a. 120-cell
   b. Window
   c. 2-3 heap
   d. 1-center problem

13. An _____ of a real-valued function y = f(x) is a curve which describes the behavior of f as either x or y tends to infinity.

In other words, as one moves along the graph of f(x) in some direction, the distance between it and the _____ eventually becomes smaller than any distance that one may specify.

If a curve A has the curve B as an _____, one says that A is asymptotic to B. Similarly B is asymptotic to A, so A and B are called asymptotic.

   a. Isoperimetric dimension
   b. Improper integral
   c. Infinite product
   d. Asymptote

14. _____ is an algebraic technique used to solve quadratic equations, in analytic geometry for determining the shapes of graphs, and in calculus for computing integrals. The essential objective is to reduce a quadratic polynomial in a variable in an equation or expression to a squared polynomial of linear order. This can reduce an equation or integral to one that is more easily solved or evaluated.

   a. Permanent of a matrix
   b. Monomial basis
   c. Completing the square
   d. Relation algebra

15. In mathematics, the _____s are an extension of the real numbers obtained by adjoining an imaginary unit, denoted i, which satisfies:

$$i^2 = -1.$$

Every _____ can be written in the form a + bi, where a and b are real numbers called the real part and the imaginary part of the _____, respectively.

_____s are a field, and thus have addition, subtraction, multiplication, and division operations. These operations extend the corresponding operations on real numbers, although with a number of additional elegant and useful properties, e.g., negative real numbers can be obtained by squaring _____s.

   a. 120-cell
   b. Complex number
   c. Real part
   d. 1-center problem

16. A _____ is the longest side of a right triangle, the side opposite of the right angle. The length of the _____ of a right triangle can be found using the Pythagorean theorem, which states that the square of the length of the _____ equals the sum of the squares of the lengths of the two other sides.

For example, if one of the other sides has a length of 3 meters and the other has a length of 4 m.

a. Golden angle
c. Concyclic points

b. Reflection symmetry
d. Hypotenuse

17. In mathematics, the _____ of a complex number z, is the second element of the ordered pair of real numbers representing z,. It is denoted by Im or $\Im\{z\}$, where $\Im$ is a capital I in the Fraktur typeface. The complex function which maps z to the _____ of z is not holomorphic.

a. Imaginary part
c. A posteriori

b. A Mathematical Theory of Communication
d. A chemical equation

18. In mathematics, the _____ of a complex number z, is the first element of the ordered pair of real numbers representing z. It is denoted by Re{z} or $\Re\{z\}$, where $\Re$ is a capital R in the Fraktur typeface. The complex function which maps z to the _____ of z is not holomorphic.

a. 1-center problem
c. Real part

b. 120-cell
d. Complex number

19. A _____ typically refers to a class of handheld calculators that are capable of plotting graphs, solving simultaneous equations, and performing numerous other tasks with variables. Most popular _____s are also programmable, allowing the user to create customized programs, typically for scientific/engineering and education applications. Due to their large displays intended for graphing, they can also accommodate several lines of text and calculations at a time.

a. Bump mapping
c. Graphing calculator

b. Support vector machines
d. Genus

20. In mathematics, an _____ is a complex number whose squared value is a real number less than or equal to zero. The imaginary unit, denoted by i or j, is an example of an _____. If y is a real number, then i·y is an _____, because:

$$(i \cdot y)^2 = i^2 \cdot y^2 = -y^2 \leq 0.$$

They were defined in 1572 by Rafael Bombelli.

a. Imaginary number
c. A posteriori

b. A chemical equation
d. A Mathematical Theory of Communication

21. In mathematics, the _____ of a real number is its numerical value without regard to its sign. So, for example, 3 is the _____ of both 3 and −3.

The _____ of a number a is denoted by $|a|$.

Generalizations of the _____ for real numbers occur in a wide variety of mathematical settings.

a. A Mathematical Theory of Communication
c. Area hyperbolic functions

b. A chemical equation
d. Absolute value

Chapter 3. Functions, Equations, and Inequalities

22. In mathematics, _____ is a property that a binary operation can have. It means that, within an expression containing two or more of the same associative operators in a row, the order that the operations are performed does not matter as long as the sequence of the operands is not changed. That is, rearranging the parentheses in such an expression will not change its value.

   a. Idempotence
   b. Algebraically closed
   c. Unital
   d. Associativity

23. A _____ is a device for performing mathematical calculations, distinguished from a computer by having a limited problem solving ability and an interface optimized for interactive calculation rather than programming. _____s can be hardware or software, and mechanical or electronic, and are often built into devices such as PDAs or mobile phones.

   Modern electronic _____s are generally small, digital, and usually inexpensive.

   a. 1-center problem
   b. 2-3 heap
   c. 120-cell
   d. Calculator

24. In mathematics, the _____ of a complex number is given by changing the sign of the imaginary part. Thus, the conjugate of the complex number

$$z = a + ib$$

(where a and b are real numbers) is

$$\bar{z} = a - ib.$$

The _____ is also very commonly denoted by z * . Here $\bar{z}$ is chosen to avoid confusion with the notation for the conjugate transpose of a matrix (which can be thought of as a generalization of complex conjugation.)

   a. Real part
   b. 120-cell
   c. Complex conjugate
   d. 1-center problem

25. In algebra, a _____ of an element in a quadratic extension field of a field K is its image under the unique non-identity automorphism of the extended field that fixes K. If the extension is generated by a square root of an element r of K, then the _____ of $a + b\sqrt{r}$ is $a - b\sqrt{r}$ for $a, b \in K$, and in particular in the case of the field C of complex numbers as an extension of the field R of real numbers, the complex _____ of a + bi is a − bi.

   Forming the sum or product of any element of the extension field with its _____ always gives an element of K.

   a. Conjugate
   b. Trinomial
   c. Relation algebra
   d. Real structure

26. In mathematics, the _____ is a conic section, the intersection of a right circular conical surface and a plane parallel to a generating straight line of that surface. Given a point and a line that lie in a plane, the locus of points in that plane that are equidistant to them is a _____.

A particular case arises when the plane is tangent to the conical surface of a circle.

a. Directrix
b. Dandelin sphere
c. Matrix representation of conic sections
d. Parabola

27. In mathematics, a _____ is a polynomial equation of the second degree. The general form is

$$ax^2 + bx + c = 0,$$

where a ≠ 0.

The letters a, b, and c are called coefficients: the quadratic coefficient a is the coefficient of x^2, the linear coefficient b is the coefficient of x, and c is the constant coefficient, also called the free term or constant term.

a. Quartic equation
b. Difference of two squares
c. Linear equation
d. Quadratic equation

28. A _____, in mathematics, is a polynomial function of the form $f(x) = ax^2 + bx + c$, where $a \neq 0$. The graph of a _____ is a parabola whose major axis is parallel to the y-axis.

The expression $ax^2 + bx + c$ in the definition of a _____ is a polynomial of degree 2 or a 2nd degree polynomial, because the highest exponent of x is 2.

a. Multivariate division algorithm
b. Discriminant
c. Laguerre polynomials
d. Quadratic function

29. In vascular plants, the _____ is the organ of a plant body that typically lies below the surface of the soil. This is not always the case, however, since a _____ can also be aerial (that is, growing above the ground) or aerating (that is, growing up above the ground or especially above water.) Furthermore, a stem normally occurring below ground is not exceptional either

a. Root
b. 1-center problem
c. 120-cell
d. 2-3 heap

30. _____, also sometimes known as standard form or as exponential notation, is a way of writing numbers that accommodates values too large or small to be conveniently written in standard decimal notation. _____ has a number of useful properties and is often favored by scientists, mathematicians and engineers, who work with such numbers.

In _____, numbers are written in the form:

$$a \times 10^b$$

a. Leading zero
c. 1-center problem
b. Radix point
d. Scientific notation

31. A _____ is a simple shape of Euclidean geometry consisting of those points in a plane which are at a constant distance, called the radius, from a fixed point, called the center. A _____ with center A is sometimes denoted by the symbol A.

A chord of a _____ is a line segment whose two endpoints lie on the _____.

a. Malfatti circles
c. Circumcircle
b. Circular segment
d. Circle

32. In algebra, the _____ of a polynomial with real or complex coefficients is a certain expression in the coefficients of the polynomial which is equal to zero if and only if the polynomial has a multiple root in the complex numbers. For example, the _____ of the quadratic polynomial

$$ax^2 + bx + c \text{ is } b^2 - 4ac.$$

The _____ of the cubic polynomial

$$ax^3 + bx^2 + cx + d \text{ is } b^2c^2 - 4ac^3 - 4b^3d - 27a^2d^2 + 18abcd.$$

a. Square-free polynomial
c. Discriminant
b. Boubaker polynomial
d. Jacobian conjecture

33. In mathematics, a _____ of a number x is a number r such that $r^2 = x$, or, in other words, a number r whose square is x. Every non-negative real number x has a unique non-negative _____, called the principal _____, which is denoted with a radical symbol as $\sqrt{x}$, or, using exponent notation, as $x^{1/2}$. For example, the principal _____ of 9 is 3, denoted $\sqrt{9} = 3$, because $3^2 = 3 \times 3 = 9$.

a. Double exponential
c. Hyperbolic functions
b. Multiplicative inverse
d. Square root

34. A quadratic equation with real solutions, called roots, which may be real or complex, is given by the _____: $x = \frac{-b \pm \sqrt{b^2 - 4ac}}{2a}$.

a. Parametric continuity
c. Quadratic formula
b. Quotient
d. Differential Algebra

35. If ε is a vector of n random variables, and Λ is an n-dimensional symmetric square matrix, then the scalar quantity ε'Λε is known as a _____ in ε.

It can be shown that

$$E\left[\epsilon'\Lambda\epsilon\right] = \operatorname{tr}\left[\Lambda\Sigma\right] + \mu'\Lambda\mu$$

Chapter 3. Functions, Equations, and Inequalities 43

where μ and Σ are the expected value and variance-covariance matrix of ε, respectively, and tr denotes the trace of a matrix. This result only depends on the existence of μ and Σ; in particular, normality of ε is not required.

- a. Complex conjugate vector space
- b. Field of values
- c. Gram-Schmidt process
- d. Quadratic form

36. In computational complexity theory, an algorithm is said to take _____ if the asymptotic upper bound for the time it requires is proportional to the size of the input, which is usually denoted n.

Informally spoken, the running time increases linearly with the size of the input. For example, a procedure that adds up all elements of a list requires time proportional to the length of the list.

- a. Constructible function
- b. Linear time
- c. Truth table reduction
- d. Time-constructible function

37. In mathematics, a group G is called _____ if there is a subset S of G such that any element of G can be written in one and only one way as a product of finitely many elements of S and their inverses.

A related but different notion is a _____ abelian group.

_____ groups first arose in the study of hyperbolic geometry, as examples of Fuchsian groups.

- a. Boolean algebra
- b. Leibniz formula
- c. Barycentric coordinates
- d. Free

38. _____ generally conveys two primary meanings. The first is an imprecise sense of harmonious or aesthetically-pleasing proportionality and balance; such that it reflects beauty or perfection. The second meaning is a precise and well-defined concept of balance or 'patterned self-similarity' that can be demonstrated or proved according to the rules of a formal system: by geometry, through physics or otherwise.

- a. Tessellation
- b. Molecular symmetry
- c. Symmetry breaking
- d. Symmetry

39. In geometry, a _____ is a special kind of point, usually a corner of a polygon, polyhedron, or higher dimensional polytope. In the geometry of curves a _____ is a point of where the first derivative of curvature is zero. In graph theory, a _____ is the fundamental unit out of which graphs are formed

- a. Crib
- b. Duality
- c. Vertex
- d. Dini

40. In geometry and trigonometry, an _____ is the figure formed by two rays sharing a common endpoint, called the vertex of the _____. The magnitude of the _____ is the 'amount of rotation' that separates the two rays, and can be measured by considering the length of circular arc swept out when one ray is rotated about the vertex to coincide with the other. Where there is no possibility of confusion, the term '_____' is used interchangeably for both the geometric configuration itself and for its angular magnitude.

Chapter 3. Functions, Equations, and Inequalities

a. A chemical equation
b. Angle
c. A posteriori
d. A Mathematical Theory of Communication

41. In mathematics, _____ is a technique for optimization of a linear objective function, subject to linear equality and linear inequality constraints. Informally, _____ determines the way to achieve the best outcome in a given mathematical model given some list of requirements represented as linear equations.

More formally, given a polytope, and a real-valued affine function

$$f(x_1, x_2, \ldots, x_n) = c_1 x_1 + c_2 x_2 + \cdots + c_n x_n + d$$

defined on this polytope, a _____ method will find a point in the polytope where this function has the smallest value.

a. Descent direction
b. Linear programming
c. Lin-Kernighan
d. Linear programming relaxation

42. In descriptive statistics, the _____ is the length of the smallest interval which contains all the data. It is calculated by subtracting the smallest observations from the greatest and provides an indication of statistical dispersion.

It is measured in the same units as the data.

a. Kernel
b. Bandwidth
c. Class
d. Range

43. In economics, business, retail, and accounting, a _____ is the value of money that has been used up to produce something, and hence is not available for use anymore. In business, the _____ may be one of acquisition, in which case the amount of money expended to acquire it is counted as _____. In this case, money is the input that is gone in order to acquire the thing.

a. 1-center problem
b. 120-cell
c. 2-3 heap
d. Cost

44. In mathematics, an algebraic group G contains a unique maximal normal solvable subgroup; and this subgroup is closed. Its identity component is called the _____ of G.

a. Radical
b. Barycentric coordinates
c. Block size
d. Composite

45. A _____ is an expression containing a square root.

a. Convolution
b. Controlled Cryptographic Item
c. Convolution theorem
d. Radical expression

46. In mathematics, and more specifically set theory, the _____ is the unique set having no members. Some axiomatic set theories assure that the _____ exists by including an axiom of _____; in other theories, its existence can be deduced. Many possible properties of sets are trivially true for the _____.

Chapter 3. Functions, Equations, and Inequalities   45

a. Inverse function
b. Empty function
c. A Mathematical Theory of Communication
d. Empty set

47.   In mathematics, an _____ or member of a set is any one of the distinct objects that make up that set.

Writing A = {1,2,3,4}, means that the _____s of the set A are the numbers 1, 2, 3 and 4. Groups of _____s of A, for example {1,2}, are subsets of A.

a. Element
b. Universal code
c. Ideal
d. Order

48.   In mathematics, an _____ is a statement about the relative size or order of two objects, or about whether they are the same or not

- The notation a < b means that a is less than b.
- The notation a > b means that a is greater than b.
- The notation a ≠ b means that a is not equal to b, but does not say that one is bigger than the other or even that they can be compared in size.

In all these cases, a is not equal to b, hence, '_____'.

These relations are known as strict _____

- The notation a ≤ b means that a is less than or equal to b;
- The notation a ≥ b means that a is greater than or equal to b;

An additional use of the notation is to show that one quantity is much greater than another, normally by several orders of magnitude.

- The notation a << b means that a is much less than b.
- The notation a >> b means that a is much greater than b.

If the sense of the _____ is the same for all values of the variables for which its members are defined, then the _____ is called an 'absolute' or 'unconditional' _____. If the sense of an _____ holds only for certain values of the variables involved, but is reversed or destroyed for other values of the variables, it is called a conditional _____.

An _____ may appear unsolvable because it only states whether a number is larger or smaller than another number; but it is possible to apply the same operations for equalities to inequalities. For example, to find x for the _____ 10x > 23 one would divide 23 by 10.

a. A Mathematical Theory of Communication
b. A chemical equation
c. Inequality
d. A posteriori

49. In logic and mathematics, or, also known as logical _____ or inclusive _____ is a logical operator that results in true whenever one or more of its operands are true. In grammar, or is a coordinating conjunction. In ordinary language 'or' rather has the meaning of exclusive _____.
   a. Zero-point energy   b. Triquetra
   c. Disjunction   d. Cube

50. In set theory, the term _____ refers to a set operation used in the convergence of set elements to form a resultant set containing the elements of both sets. As a simple example, a _____ of two disjoint sets, which do not have elements in common results in a set containing all elements from both sets. A Venn diagram representing the _____ of sets A and B.
   a. Event   b. Introduction
   c. UES   d. Union

Chapter 4. Polynomial and Rational Functions

1. In mathematics, a _____ is a constant multiplicative factor of a certain object. For example, in the expression $9x^2$, the _____ of x^2 is 9.

   The object can be such things as a variable, a vector, a function, etc.

   a. Multivariate division algorithm
   b. Stability radius
   c. Fibonacci polynomials
   d. Coefficient

2. In mathematics, a _____ is a function whose values do not vary and thus are constant. For example, if we have the function f→ B is a _____ if f
   a. Squeeze mapping
   b. Point reflection
   c. Linear operator
   d. Constant function

3. In mathematics, a _____ is a function of the form

   $f3 + bx^2 + cx + d$,

   where a is nonzero; or in other words, a polynomial of degree three. The derivative of a _____ is a quadratic function. The integral of a _____ is a quartic function.

   a. Cubic function
   b. Linear equation
   c. Quadratic equation
   d. Quartic equation

4. The mathematical concept of a _____ expresses the intuitive idea of deterministic dependence between two quantities, one of which is viewed as primary and the other as secondary. A _____ then is a way to associate a unique output for each input of a specified type, for example, a real number or an element of a given set.
   a. Grill
   b. Coherent
   c. Going up
   d. Function

5. In mathematics, a _____ is an expression constructed from variables and constants, using the operations of addition, subtraction, multiplication, and constant non-negative whole number exponents. For example, $x^2 - 4x + 7$ is a _____, but $x^2 - 4/x + 7x^{3/2}$ is not, because its second term involves division by the variable x and also because its third term contains an exponent that is not a whole number.

   _____s are one of the most important concepts in algebra and throughout mathematics and science.

   a. Polynomial
   b. Semifield
   c. Coimage
   d. Group extension

6. A _____, in mathematics, is a polynomial function of the form $f(x) = ax^2 + bx + c$, where $a \neq 0$. The graph of a _____ is a parabola whose major axis is parallel to the y-axis.

   The expression $ax^2 + bx + c$ in the definition of a _____ is a polynomial of degree 2 or a 2nd degree polynomial, because the highest exponent of x is 2.

a. Laguerre polynomials
c. Multivariate division algorithm

b. Discriminant
d. Quadratic function

7. In mathematics, a _____ of a set X is a collection of sets such that X is a subset of the union of sets in the collection. In symbols, if

$$C = \{U_\alpha : \alpha \in A\}$$

is an indexed family of sets U_α, then C is a _____ of X if

$$X \subseteq \bigcup_{\alpha \in A} U_\alpha$$

_____s are commonly used in the context of topology. If the set X is a topological space, then a _____ C of X is a collection of subsets U_α of X whose union is the whole space X.

a. Generalised metric
c. Manifold

b. Contractible space
d. Cover

8. In probability theory, a probability distribution is called _____ if its cumulative distribution function is _____. That is equivalent to saying that for random variables X with the distribution in question, Pr[X = a] = 0 for all real numbers a. If the distribution of X is _____ then X is called a _____ random variable.

a. Continuous phase modulation
c. Conull set

b. Concatenated codes
d. Continuous

9. In mathematics, a _____ is a function for which, intuitively, small changes in the input result in small changes in the output. Otherwise, a function is said to be discontinuous. A _____ with a continuous inverse function is called bicontinuous.

a. Charles's Law
c. Contraction mapping

b. Beth numbers
d. Continuous function

10. In mathematics, especially in the area of abstract algebra known as ring theory, a _____ is a ring with 0 ≠ 1 such that ab = 0 implies that either a = 0 or b = 0. That is, it is a nontrivial ring without left or right zero divisors. A commutative _____ is called an integral _____.

a. Simple ring
c. Left primitive ring

b. Modular representation theory
d. Domain

11. An _____ of a real-valued function y = f(x) is a curve which describes the behavior of f as either x or y tends to infinity.

In other words, as one moves along the graph of f(x) in some direction, the distance between it and the _____ eventually becomes smaller than any distance that one may specify.

If a curve A has the curve B as an _____, one says that A is asymptotic to B. Similarly B is asymptotic to A, so A and B are called asymptotic.

a. Asymptote
b. Infinite product
c. Isoperimetric dimension
d. Improper integral

12. In mathematics, a _____ on a fiber bundle is a device that defines a notion of parallel transport on the bundle; that is, a way to 'connect' or identify fibers over nearby points. If the fiber bundle is a vector bundle, then the notion of parallel transport is required to be linear. Such a _____ is equivalently specified by a covariant derivative, which is an operator that can differentiate sections of that bundle along tangent directions in the base manifold.
   a. 120-cell
   b. 1-center problem
   c. Connectivity
   d. Connection

13. In mathematical analysis, the _____ states that for each value between the least upper bound and greatest lower bound of the image of a continuous function there is a corresponding value in its domain mapping to the original. _____

   - Version I. The _____ states the following: If the function y = f∈ [a, b] such that f

   - Version II. Suppose that I is an interval [a, b] in the real numbers R and that f : I → R is a continuous function. Then the image set f

   f⊇ [f or f(I) ⊇ [f(b), f(a)].

It is frequently stated in the following equivalent form: Suppose that f : [a, b] → R is continuous and that u is a real number satisfying f(a) < u < f(b) or f(a) > u > f(b).) Then for some c ∈ [a, b], f(c) = u.

This captures an intuitive property of continuous functions: given f continuous on [1, 2], if f(1) = 3 and f(2) = 5 then f must take the value 4 somewhere between 1 and 2.

   a. A Mathematical Theory of Communication
   b. Equicontinuous
   c. Intermediate value theorem
   d. Uniformly continuous

14. In mathematics, a _____ is a statement that can be proved on the basis of explicitly stated or previously agreed assumptions.
   a. Logical value
   b. Boolean function
   c. Disjunction introduction
   d. Theorem

15. A _____ is an abstract model that uses mathematical language to describe the behavior of a system. Eykhoff defined a _____ as 'a representation of the essential aspects of an existing system which presents knowledge of that system in usable form'.
   a. Rata Die
   b. Metaheuristic
   c. Total least squares
   d. Mathematical model

16. In ecology, predation describes a biological interaction where a _____ (an organism that is hunting) feeds on its prey, the organism that is attacked. _____s may or may not kill their prey prior to feeding on them, but the act of predation always results in the death of the prey. The other main category of consumption is detritivory, the consumption of dead organic material (detritus.)

a. Prey
b. 1-center problem
c. 120-cell
d. Predator

17. In mathematics, the concept of a _____ tries to capture the intuitive idea of a geometrical one-dimensional and continuous object. A simple example is the circle. In everyday use of the term '_____', a straight line is not curved, but in mathematical parlance _____s include straight lines and line segments.
   a. Quadrifolium
   b. Kappa curve
   c. Negative pedal curve
   d. Curve

18. _____ is finding a curve which has the best fit to a series of data points and possibly other constraints. This section is an introduction to both interpolation and regression analysis. Both are sometimes used for extrapolation.
   a. Numerical stability
   b. Curve fitting
   c. Multiphysics
   d. Spectral methods

19. The _____ is a unit of plane angle, equal to 180/π degrees, or about 57.2958 degrees. It is the standard unit of angular measurement in all areas of mathematics beyond the elementary level.

   The _____ is represented by the symbol 'rad' or, more rarely, by the superscript c.

   a. 120-cell
   b. 1-center problem
   c. 2-3 heap
   d. RADIAN

20. The _____ fallacy is an informal fallacy. It ascribes cause where none exists. The flaw is failing to account for natural fluctuations.
   a. Degrees of freedom
   b. Depth
   c. Differential
   d. Regression

21. In statistics, the _____ is the value that occurs the most frequently in a data set or a probability distribution. In some fields, notably education, sample data are often called scores, and the sample _____ is known as the modal score.

   Like the statistical mean and the median, the _____ is a way of capturing important information about a random variable or a population in a single quantity.

   a. Mode
   b. Field
   c. Deltoid
   d. Function

22. A _____ is a structured activity, usually undertaken for enjoyment and sometimes also used as an educational tool. _____s are distinct from work, which is usually carried out for remuneration, and from art, which is more concerned with the expression of ideas. However, the distinction is not clear-cut, and many _____s are also considered to be work (such as professional players of spectator sports/_____s) or art (such as jigsaw puzzles or _____s involving an artistic layout such as Mah-jongg solitaire.)
   a. 2-3 heap
   b. 1-center problem
   c. 120-cell
   d. Game

Chapter 4. Polynomial and Rational Functions

23. In computational complexity theory, an algorithm is said to take _____ if the asymptotic upper bound for the time it requires is proportional to the size of the input, which is usually denoted n.

Informally spoken, the running time increases linearly with the size of the input. For example, a procedure that adds up all elements of a list requires time proportional to the length of the list.

a. Linear time
b. Time-constructible function
c. Truth table reduction
d. Constructible function

24. In the physical sciences, _____ is a measurement of the gravitational force acting on an object. Near the surface of the Earth, the acceleration due to gravity is approximately constant; this means that an object's _____ is roughly proportional to its mass.

In commerce and in many other applications, _____ means the same as mass as that term is used in physics.

a. 1-center problem
b. 2-3 heap
c. 120-cell
d. Weight

25. In ring theory, a branch of abstract algebra, an _____ is a special subset of a ring. The _____ concept generalizes in an appropriate way some important properties of integers like 'even number' or 'multiple of 3'.

For instance, in rings one studies prime _____ s instead of prime numbers, one defines coprime _____ s as a generalization of coprime numbers, and one can prove a generalized Chinese remainder theorem about _____ s.

a. Ideal
b. Equaliser
c. Element
d. Equity

26. In mathematics, the _____ s are an extension of the real numbers obtained by adjoining an imaginary unit, denoted i, which satisfies:

$$i^2 = -1.$$

Every _____ can be written in the form a + bi, where a and b are real numbers called the real part and the imaginary part of the _____, respectively.

_____ s are a field, and thus have addition, subtraction, multiplication, and division operations. These operations extend the corresponding operations on real numbers, although with a number of additional elegant and useful properties, e.g., negative real numbers can be obtained by squaring _____ s.

a. 120-cell
b. Real part
c. Complex number
d. 1-center problem

Chapter 4. Polynomial and Rational Functions

27. _____s are payments made by a corporation to its shareholder members. When a corporation earns a profit or surplus, that money can be put to two uses: it can either be re-invested in the business, or it can be paid to the shareholders as a _____. Many corporations retain a portion of their earnings and pay the remainder as a _____.

a. GNU Privacy Guard
b. 120-cell
c. 1-center problem
d. Dividend

28. In mathematics, a _____ of an integer n is an integer which evenly divides n without leaving a remainder.

For example, 7 is a _____ of 42 because 42/7 = 6. We also say 42 is divisible by 7 or 42 is a multiple of 7 or 7 divides 42 or 7 is a factor of 42 and we usually write 7 | 42.

a. 1-center problem
b. 120-cell
c. 2-3 heap
d. Divisor

29. In mathematics, a _____ is the end result of a division problem. It can also be expressed as the number of times the divisor divides into the dividend.

a. Marginal cost
b. Quotient
c. Notation
d. Limiting

30. In mathematics, the _____ states that every non-constant single-variable polynomial with complex coefficients has at least one complex root. Equivalently, the field of complex numbers is algebraically closed.

Sometimes, this theorem is stated as: every non-zero single-variable polynomial, with complex coefficients, has exactly as many complex roots as its degree, if each root is counted up to its multiplicity.

a. Near-semiring
b. Fundamental theorem of algebra
c. Closure with a twist
d. Distributive

31. In algebra, a _____ of an element in a quadratic extension field of a field K is its image under the unique non-identity automorphism of the extended field that fixes K. If the extension is generated by a square root of an element r of K, then the _____ of $a + b\sqrt{r}$ is $a - b\sqrt{r}$ for $a, b \in K$, and in particular in the case of the field C of complex numbers as an extension of the field R of real numbers, the complex _____ of a + bi is a − bi.

Forming the sum or product of any element of the extension field with its _____ always gives an element of K.

a. Relation algebra
b. Real structure
c. Conjugate
d. Trinomial

32. In mathematics, a _____ is any function which can be written as the ratio of two polynomial functions. _____ of degree 2 :

$$y = \frac{x^2 - 3x - 2}{x^2 - 4}$$

In the case of one variable, x, a _____ is a function of the form

$$f(x) = \frac{P(x)}{Q(x)}$$

where P and Q are polynomial function in x and Q is not the zero polynomial. The domain of f is the set of all points x for which the denominator Q

a. Legendre rational functions
c. 120-cell

b. 1-center problem
d. Rational function

33. The _____ is a function in mathematics. The application of this function to a value x is written as ex. Equivalently, this can be written in the form e^x, where e is a mathematical constant, the base of the natural logarithm, which equals approximately 2.718281828, and is also known as Euler's number.

a. Exponential function
c. A Mathematical Theory of Communication

b. Area hyperbolic functions
d. A chemical equation

34. Suppose f is a function. Then the line y = a is a _____ for f if

$$\lim_{x \to \infty} f(x) = a \quad \text{or} \quad \lim_{x \to -\infty} f(x) = a.$$

Intuitively, this means that f(x) can be made as close as desired to a by making x big enough. How big is big enough depends on how close one wishes to make f(x) to a.

a. 2-3 heap
c. Horizontal asymptote

b. 120-cell
d. 1-center problem

35. When a linear asymptote is not parallel to the x- or y-axis, it is called either an oblique asymptote or equivalently a _____. The function f(x) is asymptotic to y = mx + b if

$$\lim_{x \to \infty} f(x) - (mx + b) = 0 \quad \text{or} \quad \lim_{x \to -\infty} f(x) - (mx + b) = 0$$

Note that y = mx + b is never a vertical asymptote, but can be a horizontal asymptote if m=0 (in which case it is not an oblique asymptote.)

An example is $f(x)=(x^2-1)/x$ which has an oblique asymptote of y=x (m=1, b=0) as seen in the limit

$$\lim_{x \to \infty} f(x) - x$$
$$= \lim_{x \to \infty} \frac{x^2 - 1}{x} - x$$
$$= \lim_{x \to \infty} (x - 1/x) - x$$
$$= \lim_{x \to \infty} -1/x = 0$$

Computationally identifying an oblique asymptote can be more difficult than a horizontal or vertical asymptote, in particular because the m and b might not be known.

a. 2-3 heap
b. 120-cell
c. 1-center problem
d. Slant asymptote

36. In mathematics, an _____ is a statement about the relative size or order of two objects, or about whether they are the same or not

- The notation a < b means that a is less than b.
- The notation a > b means that a is greater than b.
- The notation a ≠ b means that a is not equal to b, but does not say that one is bigger than the other or even that they can be compared in size.

In all these cases, a is not equal to b, hence, '_____'.

These relations are known as strict _____

- The notation a ≤ b means that a is less than or equal to b;
- The notation a ≥ b means that a is greater than or equal to b;

An additional use of the notation is to show that one quantity is much greater than another, normally by several orders of magnitude.

- The notation a << b means that a is much less than b.
- The notation a >> b means that a is much greater than b.

If the sense of the _____ is the same for all values of the variables for which its members are defined, then the _____ is called an 'absolute' or 'unconditional' _____. If the sense of an _____ holds only for certain values of the variables involved, but is reversed or destroyed for other values of the variables, it is called a conditional _____.

Chapter 4. Polynomial and Rational Functions

An _____ may appear unsolvable because it only states whether a number is larger or smaller than another number; but it is possible to apply the same operations for equalities to inequalities. For example, to find x for the _____ 10x > 23 one would divide 23 by 10.

a. A Mathematical Theory of Communication
b. Inequality
c. A posteriori
d. A chemical equation

37. In differential topology, a _____ of a differentiable function between differentiable manifolds is the image of a critical point.

The basic result on _____s is Sard's lemma. The set of _____s can be quite irregular; but in Morse theory it becomes important to consider real-valued functions on a manifold M, such that the set of _____s is in fact finite.

a. Laplacian vector field
b. Critical value
c. Toeplitz operator
d. Spectral set

38. In mathematics and in the sciences, a _____ (plural: _____e, formulæ or _____s) is a concise way of expressing information symbolically (as in a mathematical or chemical _____), or a general relationship between quantities. One of many famous _____e is Albert Einstein's $E = mc^2$ (see special relativity

In mathematics, a _____ is a key to solve an equation with variables. For example, the problem of determining the volume of a sphere is one that requires a significant amount of integral calculus to solve.

a. 1-center problem
b. 2-3 heap
c. Formula
d. 120-cell

39. In geometry a _____ is traditionally a plane figure that is bounded by a closed path or circuit, composed of a finite sequence of straight line segments. These segments are called its edges or sides, and the points where two edges meet are the _____'s vertices or corners. The interior of the _____ is sometimes called its body.

a. Polygon
b. Polygonal curve
c. Parallelogon
d. Regular polygon

40. In mathematics, two quantities are called _____ if they vary in such a way that one of the quantities is a constant multiple of the other, or equivalently if they have a constant ratio.

a. 2-3 heap
b. 120-cell
c. 1-center problem
d. Proportional

41. _____ is a special mathematical relationship between two quantities. Two quantities are called proportional if they vary in such a way that one of the quantities is a constant multiple of the other, or equivalently if they have a constant ratio.

a. Proportionality
b. Discontinuity
c. Depth
d. Compression

42. In mathematics, the _____ of a number n is the number that, when added to n, yields zero. The _____ of n is denoted −n. For example, 7 is −7, because 7 + (−7) = 0, and the _____ of −0.3 is 0.3, because −0.3 + 0.3 = 0.
   a. Algebraic structure
   b. Associativity
   c. Arity
   d. Additive inverse

43. In combinatorial mathematics, a _____ is an un-ordered collection of distinct elements, usually of a prescribed size and taken from a given set. Given such a set S, a _____ of elements of S is just a subset of S, where as always forsets the order of the elements is not taken into account. Also, as always forsets, no elements can be repeated more than once in a _____; this is often referred to as a 'collection without repetition'.
   a. Combination
   b. Heawood number
   c. Fill-in
   d. Sparsity

44. In several fields of mathematics the term _____ is used with different but closely related meanings. They all relate to the notion of mapping the elements of a set to other elements of the same set, i.e., exchanging elements of a set.

The general concept of _____ can be defined more formally in different contexts:

In combinatorics, a _____ is usually understood to be a sequence containing each element from a finite set once, and only once.

   a. Cyclic permutation
   b. Linearly independent
   c. Tensor product
   d. Permutation

Chapter 5. Exponential and Logarithmic Functions

1. In mathematics, the _____ of a number n is the number that, when added to n, yields zero. The _____ of n is denoted −n. For example, 7 is −7, because 7 + (−7) = 0, and the _____ of −0.3 is 0.3, because −0.3 + 0.3 = 0.
   a. Arity
   b. Additive inverse
   c. Associativity
   d. Algebraic structure

2. An _____ of a real-valued function y = f(x) is a curve which describes the behavior of f as either x or y tends to infinity.

   In other words, as one moves along the graph of f(x) in some direction, the distance between it and the _____ eventually becomes smaller than any distance that one may specify.

   If a curve A has the curve B as an _____, one says that A is asymptotic to B. Similarly B is asymptotic to A, so A and B are called asymptotic.

   a. Improper integral
   b. Infinite product
   c. Isoperimetric dimension
   d. Asymptote

3. The mathematical concept of a _____ expresses the intuitive idea of deterministic dependence between two quantities, one of which is viewed as primary and the other as secondary. A _____ then is a way to associate a unique output for each input of a specified type, for example, a real number or an element of a given set.
   a. Grill
   b. Going up
   c. Coherent
   d. Function

4. _____ is a branch of mathematics which focuses on the study of matrices. Initially a sub-branch of linear algebra, it has grown to cover subjects related to graph theory, algebra, combinatorics, and statistics as well.

   The term matrix was first coined in 1848 by J.J. Sylvester as a name of an array of numbers.

   a. Segre classification
   b. Pairing
   c. Semi-simple operators
   d. Matrix theory

5. An injective function is called an injection, and is also said to be a _____ (not to be confused with one-to-one correspondence, i.e. a bijective function.)

   A function f that is not injective is sometimes called many-to-one. (However, this terminology is also sometimes used to mean 'single-valued', i.e. each argument is mapped to at most one value.)

   a. A Mathematical Theory of Communication
   b. A posteriori
   c. A chemical equation
   d. One-to-one function

6. In elementary algebra, a _____ is a polynomial with two terms: the sum of two monomials. It is the simplest kind of polynomial except for a monomial.

Chapter 5. Exponential and Logarithmic Functions

The _____ $a^2 - b^2$ can be factored as the product of two other _____s:

$a^2 - b^2$.

The product of a pair of linear _____s $ax + b$ and $cx + d$ is:

$2 + x + bd$.

A _____ raised to the nth power, represented as

n

can be expanded by means of the _____ theorem or, equivalently, using Pascal's triangle.

- a. Real structure
- b. Cylindrical algebraic decomposition
- c. Binomial
- d. Rational root theorem

7. In mathematics, the _____ $\binom{n}{k}$ is the coefficient of the x^k term in the polynomial expansion of the binomial power ^{n}.

In combinatorics, $\binom{n}{k}$ is interpreted as the number of k-element subsets of an n-element set, that is the number of ways that k things can be 'chosen' from a set of n things. Hence, $\binom{n}{k}$ is often read as 'n choose k' and called the choose function of n and k.

- a. Dyson conjecture
- b. Rule of product
- c. Symbolic combinatorics
- d. Binomial coefficient

8. In mathematics, a _____ is a constant multiplicative factor of a certain object. For example, in the expression $9x^2$, the _____ of x^2 is 9.

The object can be such things as a variable, a vector, a function, etc.

- a. Fibonacci polynomials
- b. Coefficient
- c. Multivariate division algorithm
- d. Stability radius

9. An _____ is a function which does the reverse of a given function.
- a. A Mathematical Theory of Communication
- b. Empty function
- c. Inverse function
- d. Empty set

10. To define the derivative of a distribution, we first consider the case of a differentiable and integrable function $f : R \to R$. If φ is a _____, then we have

Chapter 5. Exponential and Logarithmic Functions

$$\int_R f'\varphi\, dx = -\int_R f\varphi'\, dx$$

using integration by parts (note that φ is zero outside of a bounded set and that therefore no boundary values have to be taken into account.) This suggests that if S is a distribution, we should define its derivative S' by

$$\langle S', \varphi \rangle = -\langle S, \varphi' \rangle$$

a. Generalized functions
b. Schwartz kernel theorem
c. Hyperfunction
d. Test Function

11. In mathematics and in the sciences, a _____ (plural: _____e, formulæ or _____s) is a concise way of expressing information symbolically (as in a mathematical or chemical _____), or a general relationship between quantities. One of many famous _____e is Albert Einstein's E = mc² (see special relativity

In mathematics, a _____ is a key to solve an equation with variables. For example, the problem of determining the volume of a sphere is one that requires a significant amount of integral calculus to solve.

a. Formula
b. 120-cell
c. 2-3 heap
d. 1-center problem

12. In mathematics, especially in the area of abstract algebra known as ring theory, a _____ is a ring with 0 ≠ 1 such that ab = 0 implies that either a = 0 or b = 0. That is, it is a nontrivial ring without left or right zero divisors. A commutative _____ is called an integral _____.

a. Left primitive ring
b. Modular representation theory
c. Domain
d. Simple ring

13. In mathematics and computer science, _____ (also base-16, hexa or base, of 16. It uses sixteen distinct symbols, most often the symbols 0-9 to represent values zero to nine, and A, B, C, D, E, F (or a through f) to represent values ten to fifteen.

Its primary use is as a human friendly representation of binary coded values, so it is often used in digital electronics and computer engineering.

a. Factoradic
b. Hexadecimal
c. Radix
d. Tetradecimal

14. The _____ is a function in mathematics. The application of this function to a value x is written as ex. Equivalently, this can be written in the form e^x, where e is a mathematical constant, the base of the natural logarithm, which equals approximately 2.718281828, and is also known as Euler's number.

a. Area hyperbolic functions
b. Exponential function
c. A chemical equation
d. A Mathematical Theory of Communication

60 Chapter 5. Exponential andLogarithmic Functions

15. The function log_b(x) depends on both b and x, but the term _____ (or logarithmic function) in standard usage refers to a function of the form log_b(x) in which the base b is fixed and so the only argument is x. Thus there is one _____ for each value of the base b (which must be positive and must differ from 1.) Viewed in this way, the base-b _____ is the inverse function of the exponential function b^x.

   a. 1-center problem
   b. 120-cell
   c. 2-3 heap
   d. Logarithm function

16. A _____ is an opening in a wall that allows the passage of light and, if not closed or sealed, air and sound. _____s are usually glazed or covered in some other transparent or translucent material. _____s are held in place by frames, which prevent them from collapsing in.

   a. 2-3 heap
   b. 1-center problem
   c. Window
   d. 120-cell

17. _____ is the concept of adding accumulated interest back to the principal, so that interest is earned on interest from that moment on. The act of declaring interest to be principal is called compounding. A loan, for example, may have its interest compounded every month: in this case, a loan with $100 principal and 1% interest per month would have a balance of $101 at the end of the first month.

   a. Net interest margin
   b. Retained interest
   c. Compound interest
   d. Net interest margin securities

18. _____ is a fee, paid on borrowed capital. Assets lent include money, shares, consumer goods through hire purchase, major assets such as aircraft, and even entire factories in finance lease arrangements. The _____ is calculated upon the value of the assets in the same manner as upon money.

   a. Interest expense
   b. Interest sensitivity gap
   c. A Mathematical Theory of Communication
   d. Interest

19. In mathematics, a _____ on a fiber bundle is a device that defines a notion of parallel transport on the bundle; that is, a way to 'connect' or identify fibers over nearby points. If the fiber bundle is a vector bundle, then the notion of parallel transport is required to be linear. Such a _____ is equivalently specified by a covariant derivative, which is an operator that can differentiate sections of that bundle along tangent directions in the base manifold.

   a. 120-cell
   b. 1-center problem
   c. Connectivity
   d. Connection

20. In mathematics, the _____ of a number to a given base is the power or exponent to which the base must be raised in order to produce the number.

   For example, the _____ of 1000 to the base 10 is 3, because 3 is how many 10s one must multiply to get 1000: thus 10 × 10 × 10 = 1000; the base-2 _____ of 32 is 5 because 5 is how many 2s one must multiply to get 32: thus 2 × 2 × 2 × 2 × 2 = 32. In the language of exponents: 10^3 = 1000, so $\log_{10} 1000$ = 3, and 2^5 = 32, so $\log_2 32$ = 5.

   a. 120-cell
   b. 1-center problem
   c. 2-3 heap
   d. Logarithm

Chapter 5. Exponential and Logarithmic Functions

21. In descriptive statistics, the _____ is the length of the smallest interval which contains all the data. It is calculated by subtracting the smallest observations from the greatest and provides an indication of statistical dispersion.

It is measured in the same units as the data.

a. Range
c. Kernel
b. Class
d. Bandwidth

22. The _____ is the logarithm with base 10. It is also known as the decadic logarithm, named after its base. It is indicated by $\log_{10}$

a. 1-center problem
c. Logarithmic growth
b. Natural logarithm
d. Common logarithm

23. A _____ typically refers to a class of handheld calculators that are capable of plotting graphs, solving simultaneous equations, and performing numerous other tasks with variables. Most popular _____s are also programmable, allowing the user to create customized programs, typically for scientific/engineering and education applications. Due to their large displays intended for graphing, they can also accommodate several lines of text and calculations at a time.

a. Graphing calculator
c. Bump mapping
b. Support vector machines
d. Genus

24. A _____ is a device for performing mathematical calculations, distinguished from a computer by having a limited problem solving ability and an interface optimized for interactive calculation rather than programming. _____s can be hardware or software, and mechanical or electronic, and are often built into devices such as PDAs or mobile phones.

Modern electronic _____s are generally small, digital, and usually inexpensive.

a. 1-center problem
c. 120-cell
b. Calculator
d. 2-3 heap

25. The _____, formerly known as the hyperbolic logarithm, is the logarithm to the base e, where e is an irrational constant approximately equal to 2.718 281 828. It is also sometimes referred to as the Napierian logarithm, although the original meaning of this term is slightly different. In simple terms, the _____ of a number x is the power to which e would have to be raised to equal x -- for example the natural log of e itself is 1 because e^1 = e, while the _____ of 1 would be 0, since e^0 = 1.

a. Logarithmic growth
c. 1-center problem
b. Logarithmic identities
d. Natural logarithm

26. In mathematics, the _____ is an approach to finding a particular solution to certain inhomogeneous ordinary differential equations and recurrence relations. It is closely related to the annihilator method, but instead of using a particular kind of differential operator in order to find the best possible form of the particular solution, a 'guess' is made as to the appropriate form, which is then tested by differentiating the resulting equation. In this sense, the _____ is less formal but more intuitive than the annihilator method.

a. Linear differential equation
c. Differential algebraic equations
b. Method of undetermined coefficients
d. Phase line

Chapter 5. Exponential and Logarithmic Functions

27. _____ is the mathematical operation of scaling one number by another. It is one of the four basic operations in elementary arithmetic.

_____ is defined for whole numbers in terms of repeated addition; for example, 4 multiplied by 3 can be calculated by adding 3 copies of 4 together:

$$4 + 4 + 4 = 12.$$

_____ of rational numbers and real numbers is defined by systematic generalization of this basic idea.

- a. The number 0 is even.
- b. Highest common factor
- c. Least common multiple
- d. Multiplication

28. The _____ governs the differentiation of products of differentiable functions.
- a. Reciprocal Rule
- b. 120-cell
- c. 1-center problem
- d. Product rule

29. In mathematics, an arithmetic progression or _____ is a sequence of numbers such that the difference of any two successive members of the sequence is a constant. For instance, the sequence 3, 5, 7, 9, 11, 13... is an arithmetic progression with common difference 2.
- a. Edgeworth series
- b. Eisenstein series
- c. Alternating series test
- d. Arithmetic sequence

30. Exponentiation is a mathematical operation, written a^n, involving two numbers, the base a and the _____ n. When n is a positive integer, exponentiation corresponds to repeated multiplication:

$$a^n = \underbrace{a \times \cdots \times a}_{n},$$

just as multiplication by a positive integer corresponds to repeated addition:

$$a \times n = \underbrace{a + \cdots + a}_{n}.$$

The _____ is usually shown as a superscript to the right of the base. The exponentiation a^n can be read as: a raised to the n-th power, a raised to the power [of] n or possibly a raised to the _____ [of] n, or more briefly: a to the n-th power or a to the power [of] n, or even more briefly: a to the n.

- a. Exponentiating by squaring
- b. Exponent
- c. Exponential tree
- d. Exponential sum

31. This article will state and prove the _____ for differentiation, and then use it to prove these two formulas.

The _____ for differentiation states that for every natural number n, the derivative of $f(x) = x^n$ is $f'(x) = nx^{n-1}$, that is,

$$(x^n)' = nx^{n-1}.$$

The _____ for integration

$$\int x^n \, dx = \frac{x^{n+1}}{n+1} + C$$

for natural n is then an easy consequence. One just needs to take the derivative of this equality and use the _____ and linearity of differentiation on the right-hand side.

a. Standard part function
b. Periodic function
c. Power rule
d. Functional integration

32. In mathematics, a _____ is the end result of a division problem. It can also be expressed as the number of times the divisor divides into the dividend.
   a. Limiting
   b. Marginal cost
   c. Notation
   d. Quotient

33. The _____ is the period of time required for a quantity to double in size or value.
   a. Stretched exponential function
   b. Power law
   c. Doubling time
   d. Zenzizenzizenzic

34. _____ occurs when the growth rate of a mathematical function is proportional to the function's current value. In the case of a discrete domain of definition with equal intervals it is also called geometric growth or geometric decay.

With _____ of a positive value its rate of increase steadily increases, or in the case of exponential decay, its rate of decrease steadily decreases.

   a. A chemical equation
   b. Exponential growth
   c. A Mathematical Theory of Communication
   d. A posteriori

35. _____ is the change in population over time, and can be quantified as the change in the number of individuals in a population using 'per unit time' for measurement. The term _____ can technically refer to any species, but almost always refers to humans, and it is often used informally for the more specific demographic term _____ rate, and is often used to refer specifically to the growth of the population of the world.

Simple models of _____ include the Malthusian Growth Model and the logistic model.

a. 1-center problem
c. 120-cell
b. Population dynamics
d. Population growth

36. In computational complexity theory, an algorithm is said to take _____ if the asymptotic upper bound for the time it requires is proportional to the size of the input, which is usually denoted n.

Informally spoken, the running time increases linearly with the size of the input. For example, a procedure that adds up all elements of a list requires time proportional to the length of the list.

a. Time-constructible function
c. Constructible function
b. Truth table reduction
d. Linear time

37. In probability theory, a probability distribution is called _____ if its cumulative distribution function is _____. That is equivalent to saying that for random variables X with the distribution in question, Pr[X = a] = 0 for all real numbers a. If the distribution of X is _____ then X is called a _____ random variable.

a. Conull set
c. Concatenated codes
b. Continuous phase modulation
d. Continuous

38. _____ Any process by which a specified characteristic usually amplitude of the output of a device is prevented from exceeding a predetermined value.

a. Logical equivalence
c. Notation
b. Parametric continuity
d. Limiting

39. A _____ or logistic curve is the most common sigmoid curve. It models the S-curve of growth of some set P, where P might be thought of as population. The initial stage of growth is approximately exponential; then, as saturation begins, the growth slows, and at maturity, growth stops.

a. Logistic function
c. Legendre forms
b. Spin-weighted spherical harmonics
d. Jack function

40. A quantity is said to be subject to _____ if it decreases at a rate proportional to its value. Symbolically, this can be expressed as the following differential equation, where N is the quantity and λ is a positive number called the decay constant.

$$\frac{dN}{dt} = -\lambda N.$$

The solution to this equation is:

$$N(t) = N_0 e^{-\lambda t}.$$

Here is the quantity at time t, and N_0 = N is the quantity, at time t = 0.

a. Exponential integral
c. Exponential formula
b. Exponentiating by squaring
d. Exponential decay

Chapter 5. Exponential and Logarithmic Functions

41. The _____ of a quantity whose value decreases with time is the interval required for the quantity to decay to half of its initial value. The concept originated in describing how long it takes atoms to undergo radioactive decay, but also applies in a wide variety of other situations.

The term '_____' dates to 1907.

   a. Half-life
   b. Radioactive decay
   c. 120-cell
   d. 1-center problem

42. In mathematics, the concept of a _____ tries to capture the intuitive idea of a geometrical one-dimensional and continuous object. A simple example is the circle. In everyday use of the term '_____', a straight line is not curved, but in mathematical parlance _____s include straight lines and line segments.
   a. Negative pedal curve
   b. Kappa curve
   c. Quadrifolium
   d. Curve

43. _____ is finding a curve which has the best fit to a series of data points and possibly other constraints. This section is an introduction to both interpolation and regression analysis. Both are sometimes used for extrapolation.
   a. Spectral methods
   b. Curve fitting
   c. Multiphysics
   d. Numerical stability

44. A _____ is an abstract model that uses mathematical language to describe the behavior of a system. Eykhoff defined a _____ as 'a representation of the essential aspects of an existing system which presents knowledge of that system in usable form'.
   a. Metaheuristic
   b. Rata Die
   c. Total least squares
   d. Mathematical model

45. In ecology, predation describes a biological interaction where a _____ (an organism that is hunting) feeds on its prey, the organism that is attacked. _____s may or may not kill their prey prior to feeding on them, but the act of predation always results in the death of the prey. The other main category of consumption is detritivory, the consumption of dead organic material (detritus.)
   a. Predator
   b. 120-cell
   c. Prey
   d. 1-center problem

46. The _____ is a unit of plane angle, equal to 180/π degrees, or about 57.2958 degrees. It is the standard unit of angular measurement in all areas of mathematics beyond the elementary level.

The _____ is represented by the symbol 'rad' or, more rarely, by the superscript c.

   a. RADIAN
   b. 120-cell
   c. 2-3 heap
   d. 1-center problem

47. The _____ fallacy is an informal fallacy. It ascribes cause where none exists. The flaw is failing to account for natural fluctuations.
   a. Degrees of freedom
   b. Depth
   c. Differential
   d. Regression

48. In statistics, the _____ is the value that occurs the most frequently in a data set or a probability distribution. In some fields, notably education, sample data are often called scores, and the sample _____ is known as the modal score.

Like the statistical mean and the median, the _____ is a way of capturing important information about a random variable or a population in a single quantity.

   a. Function
   c. Mode
   b. Field
   d. Deltoid

49. In statistics, _____ is a model used for prediction of the probability of occurrence of an event by fitting data to a logistic curve. It makes use of several predictor variables that may be either numerical or categorical. For example, the probability that a person has a heart attack within a specified time period might be predicted from knowledge of the person's age, sex and body mass index.
   a. Median polish
   c. Statistics
   b. Skewness
   d. Logistic regression

50. _____ is an economic model describing effects on price and quantity in a market. It predicts that in a competitive market, price will function to equalize the quantity demanded by consumers, and the quantity supplied by producers, resulting in an economic equilibrium of price and quantity. The model incorporates other factors changing equilibrium as a shift of demand and/or supply.
   a. Marginal rate of substitution
   c. 1-center problem
   b. Cross price elasticity of demand
   d. Supply and demand

Chapter 6. The Trigonometric Functions

1. An angle smaller than a right angle is called an _____ (less than 90 degrees).
    a. Acute angle
    b. Euclidean geometry
    c. Ultraparallel theorem
    d. Integral geometry

2. In geometry and trigonometry, an _____ is the figure formed by two rays sharing a common endpoint, called the vertex of the _____. The magnitude of the _____ is the 'amount of rotation' that separates the two rays, and can be measured by considering the length of circular arc swept out when one ray is rotated about the vertex to coincide with the other. Where there is no possibility of confusion, the term '_____' is used interchangeably for both the geometric configuration itself and for its angular magnitude.
    a. A Mathematical Theory of Communication
    b. A chemical equation
    c. A posteriori
    d. Angle

3. The mathematical concept of a _____ expresses the intuitive idea of deterministic dependence between two quantities, one of which is viewed as primary and the other as secondary. A _____ then is a way to associate a unique output for each input of a specified type, for example, a real number or an element of a given set.
    a. Grill
    b. Coherent
    c. Going up
    d. Function

4. A _____ is the longest side of a right triangle, the side opposite of the right angle. The length of the _____ of a right triangle can be found using the Pythagorean theorem, which states that the square of the length of the _____ equals the sum of the squares of the lengths of the two other sides.

For example, if one of the other sides has a length of 3 meters and the other has a length of 4 m.

    a. Concyclic points
    b. Reflection symmetry
    c. Hypotenuse
    d. Golden angle

5. _____ is a term in mathematics. It can refer to:

    - a _____ line, in geometry
    - the trigonometric function called _____
    - the _____ method, a root-finding algorithm in numerical analysis

    a. Separable
    b. Solvable
    c. Secant
    d. Large set

6. The _____ of an angle is the ratio of the length of the opposite side to the length of the hypotenuse. In our case

$$\sin A = \frac{\text{opposite}}{\text{hypotenuse}} = \frac{a}{h}.$$

Note that this ratio does not depend on size of the particular right triangle chosen, as long as it contains the angle A, since all such triangles are similar.

The cosine of an angle is the ratio of the length of the adjacent side to the length of the hypotenuse.

a. Trigonometric functions
c. Law of sines

b. Right angle
d. Sine

7. A _____ is one of the basic shapes of geometry: a polygon with three corners or vertices and three sides or edges which are line segments. A _____ with vertices A, B, and C is denoted ABC.

In Euclidean geometry any three non-collinear points determine a unique _____ and a unique plane.

a. Triangle
c. 1-center problem

b. Fuhrmann circle
d. Kepler triangle

8. In mathematics, the _____ functions are functions of an angle; they are important when studying triangles and modeling periodic phenomena, among many other applications.

a. Trigonometric
c. Coversine

b. Gudermannian function
d. Law of sines

9. In mathematics, the _____ are functions of an angle. They are important in the study of triangles and modeling periodic phenomena, among many other applications. _____ are commonly defined as ratios of two sides of a right triangle containing the angle, and can equivalently be defined as the lengths of various line segments from a unit circle.

a. Law of sines
c. Sine

b. Trigonometric integrals
d. Trigonometric functions

10. In mathematics, the multiplicative inverse of a number x, denoted 1/x or x^{-1}, is the number which, when multiplied by x, yields 1. The multiplicative inverse of x is also called the _____ of x.

a. 120-cell
c. 2-3 heap

b. 1-center problem
d. Reciprocal

11. In trigonometry, the _____ is a function defined as tan x = $^{\sin x}/_{\cos x}$. The function is so-named because it can be defined as the length of a certain segment of a _____ (in the geometric sense) to the unit circle. In plane geometry, a line is _____ to a curve, at some point, if both line and curve pass through the point with the same direction.

a. Tangent
c. Projective connection

b. Conformal geometry
d. Hopf conjectures

12. In linear algebra, two n-by-n matrices A and B over the field K are called _____ if there exists an invertible n-by-n matrix P over K such that

$$P^{-1}AP = B.$$

One of the meanings of the term similarity transformation is such a transformation of a matrix A into a matrix B.

Similarity is an equivalence relation on the space of square matrices.

_____ matrices share many properties:

- rank
- determinant
- trace
- eigenvalues
- characteristic polynomial
- minimal polynomial
- elementary divisors

There are two reasons for these facts:

- two _____ matrices can be thought of as describing the same linear map, but with respect to different bases
- the map $X \mapsto P^{-1}XP$ is an automorphism of the associative algebra of all n-by-n matrices, as the one-object case of the above category of all matrices.

Because of this, for a given matrix A, one is interested in finding a simple 'normal form' B which is _____ to A -- the study of A then reduces to the study of the simpler matrix B.

a. Similar   b. Dense
c. Coherence   d. Blinding

13. _____ is a quantity expressing the two-dimensional size of a defined part of a surface, typically a region bounded by a closed curve. The term surface _____ refers to the total _____ of the exposed surface of a 3-dimensional solid, such as the sum of the _____s of the exposed sides of a polyhedron. _____ is an important invariant in the differential geometry of surfaces.

a. A Mathematical Theory of Communication   b. A posteriori
c. Area   d. A chemical equation

14. In mathematics, a _____ on a fiber bundle is a device that defines a notion of parallel transport on the bundle; that is, a way to 'connect' or identify fibers over nearby points. If the fiber bundle is a vector bundle, then the notion of parallel transport is required to be linear. Such a _____ is equivalently specified by a covariant derivative, which is an operator that can differentiate sections of that bundle along tangent directions in the base manifold.

a. Connection   b. 1-center problem
c. 120-cell   d. Connectivity

15. In mathematics the concept of a _____ generalizes notions such as 'length', 'area', and 'volume'. Informally, given some base set, a '_____' is any consistent assignment of 'sizes' to the subsets of the base set. Depending on the application, the 'size' of a subset may be interpreted as its physical size, the amount of something that lies within the subset, or the probability that some random process will yield a result within the subset.

a. Cusp   b. Congruent
c. Lattice   d. Measure

Chapter 6. The Trigonometric Functions

16. In statistics, the _____ is the value that occurs the most frequently in a data set or a probability distribution. In some fields, notably education, sample data are often called scores, and the sample _____ is known as the modal score.

Like the statistical mean and the median, the _____ is a way of capturing important information about a random variable or a population in a single quantity.

a. Function
b. Deltoid
c. Field
d. Mode

17. A _____ typically refers to a class of handheld calculators that are capable of plotting graphs, solving simultaneous equations, and performing numerous other tasks with variables. Most popular _____s are also programmable, allowing the user to create customized programs, typically for scientific/engineering and education applications. Due to their large displays intended for graphing, they can also accommodate several lines of text and calculations at a time.

a. Bump mapping
b. Graphing calculator
c. Support vector machines
d. Genus

18. A _____ is a device for performing mathematical calculations, distinguished from a computer by having a limited problem solving ability and an interface optimized for interactive calculation rather than programming. _____s can be hardware or software, and mechanical or electronic, and are often built into devices such as PDAs or mobile phones.

Modern electronic _____s are generally small, digital, and usually inexpensive.

a. 1-center problem
b. 120-cell
c. Calculator
d. 2-3 heap

19. In mathematics, the _____ of a number n is the number that, when added to n, yields zero. The _____ of n is denoted −n. For example, 7 is −7, because 7 + (−7) = 0, and the _____ of −0.3 is 0.3, because −0.3 + 0.3 = 0.

a. Algebraic structure
b. Associativity
c. Additive inverse
d. Arity

20. In mathematics, the _____ of a number to a given base is the power or exponent to which the base must be raised in order to produce the number.

For example, the _____ of 1000 to the base 10 is 3, because 3 is how many 10s one must multiply to get 1000: thus 10 × 10 × 10 = 1000; the base-2 _____ of 32 is 5 because 5 is how many 2s one must multiply to get 32: thus 2 × 2 × 2 × 2 × 2 = 32. In the language of exponents: 10^3 = 1000, so $\log_{10} 1000 = 3$, and $2^5 = 32$, so $\log_2 32 = 5$.

a. 120-cell
b. 2-3 heap
c. 1-center problem
d. Logarithm

21. In mathematics, a function f is _____ of a function g if f whenever A and B are complementary angles. This definition typically applies to trigonometric functions.

Chapter 6. The Trigonometric Functions

a. Cofunction
b. Boxcar function
c. Birkhoff interpolation
d. Balian-Low theorem

22. A pair of angles are complementary if the sum of their measures add up to 90 degrees.

If the two _____ are adjacent (i.e. have a common vertex and share a side, but do not have any interior points in common) their non-shared sides form a right angle.

In Euclidean geometry, the two acute angles in a right triangle are complementary, because there are 180>° in a triangle and 90>° have been accounted for by the right angle.

a. Quincunx
b. Conway polyhedron notation
c. Hypotenuse
d. Complementary angles

23. In mathematics, _____ are equalities that involve trigonometric functions that are true for every single value of the occurring variables. These identities are useful whenever expressions involving trigonometric functions need to be simplified. An important application is the integration of non-trigonometric functions: a common trick involves first using the substitution rule with a trigonometric function, and then simplifying the resulting integral with a trigonometric identity.

a. 1-center problem
b. 120-cell
c. 2-3 heap
d. Trigonometric identities

24. In mathematics, a _____ is a rectangular table of elements, which may be numbers or, more generally, any abstract quantities that can be added and multiplied. Matrices are used to describe linear equations, keep track of the coefficients of linear transformations and to record data that depend on multiple parameters. Matrices are described by the field of _____ theory.

a. Coherent
b. Double counting
c. Compression
d. Matrix

25. The Q-TIP of a geographic location is its height above a fixed reference point, often the mean sea level. _____, or geometric height, is mainly used when referring to points on the Earth's surface, while altitude or geopotential height is used for points above the surface, such as an aircraft in flight or a spacecraft in orbit.

Less commonly, _____ is measured using the center of the Earth as the reference point.

a. A Mathematical Theory of Communication
b. A posteriori
c. A chemical equation
d. Elevation

26. Initial objects are also called _____, and terminal objects are also called final.

a. Colimit
b. Direct limit
c. Terminal object
d. Coterminal

27. A _____ is a movement of an object in a circular motion. A two-dimensional object rotates around a center of _____. A three-dimensional object rotates around a line called an axis.

a. Steiner-Lehmus theorem
b. Rotation
c. Square lattice
d. Homothetic center

28. In algebraic geometry, _____ is a notion of genericity for a set of points, or other geometric objects. It means the general case situation, as opposed to some more special or coincidental cases that are possible. Its precise meaning differs in different settings.
   a. Convexity
   b. Lipschitz domain
   c. Compactness measure of a shape
   d. General position

29. In geometry, a _____ is a special kind of point, usually a corner of a polygon, polyhedron, or higher dimensional polytope. In the geometry of curves a _____ is a point of where the first derivative of curvature is zero. In graph theory, a _____ is the fundamental unit out of which graphs are formed
   a. Dini
   b. Crib
   c. Duality
   d. Vertex

30. In geometry and trigonometry, a _____ is defined as an angle between two straight intersecting lines of ninety degrees, or one-quarter of a circle.
   a. Sine integral
   b. Trigonometry
   c. Right angle
   d. Trigonometric functions

31. An angle equal to two right angles is called a _____ (equal to 180 degrees).
   a. Straight angle
   b. Theorem
   c. Loomis-Whitney inequality
   d. Householder transformation

32. A pair of angles is _____ if their measurements add up to 180 degrees. If the two _____ angles are adjacent their non-shared sides form a straight line. The supplement of 135 would be 45.
   a. Cylinder
   b. FISH
   c. Dense
   d. Supplementary

33. A _____ is a simple shape of Euclidean geometry consisting of those points in a plane which are at a constant distance, called the radius, from a fixed point, called the center. A _____ with center A is sometimes denoted by the symbol A.

A chord of a _____ is a line segment whose two endpoints lie on the _____.

   a. Circular segment
   b. Circle
   c. Circumcircle
   d. Malfatti circles

34. In mathematics, a _____ is a circle with a unit radius. Frequently, especially in trigonometry, 'the' _____ is the circle of radius 1 centered at the origin in the Cartesian coordinate system in the Euclidean plane. The _____ is often denoted S^1; the generalization to higher dimensions is the unit sphere.
   a. Inscribed angle theorem
   b. Open unit disk
   c. Excircle
   d. Unit circle

35. The _____ is a unit of plane angle, equal to 180/π degrees, or about 57.2958 degrees. It is the standard unit of angular measurement in all areas of mathematics beyond the elementary level.

The _____ is represented by the symbol 'rad' or, more rarely, by the superscript c.

Chapter 6. The Trigonometric Functions

a. 2-3 heap
b. 120-cell
c. 1-center problem
d. Radian

36. A _____ is an angle whose Line is the center of a circle, and whose sides pass through a pair of points on the circle, thereby subtending an arc between those two points whose angle is equal to the _____ itself. It is also known as the arc segment's angular distance.

On a sphere or ellipsoid, the _____ is delineated along a great circle.

a. Hypotenuse
b. Line segment
c. Central angle
d. Mirror image

37. In mathematics, the _____s are analogs of the ordinary trigonometric functions. The basic _____s are the hyperbolic sine 'sinh', and the hyperbolic cosine 'cosh', from which are derived the hyperbolic tangent 'tanh', etc., in analogy to the derived trigonometric functions. The inverse _____ are the area hyperbolic sine 'arsinh' (also called 'asinh', or sometimes by the misnomer of 'arcsinh') and so on.

a. Rectangular function
b. Hyperbolic function
c. Square root
d. Heaviside step function

38. An _____ of a real-valued function y = f(x) is a curve which describes the behavior of f as either x or y tends to infinity.

In other words, as one moves along the graph of f(x) in some direction, the distance between it and the _____ eventually becomes smaller than any distance that one may specify.

If a curve A has the curve B as an _____, one says that A is asymptotic to B. Similarly B is asymptotic to A, so A and B are called asymptotic.

a. Asymptote
b. Improper integral
c. Infinite product
d. Isoperimetric dimension

39. In mathematics, especially in the area of abstract algebra known as ring theory, a _____ is a ring with 0 ≠ 1 such that ab = 0 implies that either a = 0 or b = 0. That is, it is a nontrivial ring without left or right zero divisors. A commutative _____ is called an integral _____.

a. Domain
b. Left primitive ring
c. Modular representation theory
d. Simple ring

40. In mathematics, a _____ is a function that repeats its values after some definite period has been added to its independent variable. This property is called periodicity. An illustration of a _____ with period P.

Everyday examples are seen when the variable is time; for instance the hands of a clock or the phases of the moon show periodic behaviour.

a. Hyperbolic angle
b. Calculus controversy
c. Method of indivisibles
d. Periodic function

Chapter 6. The Trigonometric Functions

41. In descriptive statistics, the _____ is the length of the smallest interval which contains all the data. It is calculated by subtracting the smallest observations from the greatest and provides an indication of statistical dispersion.

It is measured in the same units as the data.

a. Kernel
c. Class

b. Range
d. Bandwidth

42. _____ is the magnitude of change in the oscillating variable, with each oscillation, within an oscillating system. For instance, sound waves are oscillations in atmospheric pressure and their _____s are proportional to the change in pressure during one oscillation. If the variable undergoes regular oscillations, and a graph of the system is drawn with the oscillating variable as the vertical axis and time as the horizontal axis, the _____ is visually represented by the vertical distance between the extrema of the curve.

a. Angular frequency
c. Amplitude

b. Areal velocity
d. Angular velocity

43. In mathematics, a _____ is a number that can be expressed as an integral of an algebraic function over an algebraic domain. Kontsevich and Zagier define a _____ as a complex number whose real and imaginary parts are values of absolutely convergent integrals of rational functions with rational coefficients, over domains in given by polynomial inequalities with rational coefficients.

a. Disk
c. Period

b. Closeness
d. Boussinesq approximation

44. In mathematics, an arithmetic progression or _____ is a sequence of numbers such that the difference of any two successive members of the sequence is a constant. For instance, the sequence 3, 5, 7, 9, 11, 13... is an arithmetic progression with common difference 2.

a. Eisenstein series
c. Edgeworth series

b. Arithmetic sequence
d. Alternating series test

45. In mathematics, _____ is a property that a binary operation can have. It means that, within an expression containing two or more of the same associative operators in a row, the order that the operations are performed does not matter as long as the sequence of the operands is not changed. That is, rearranging the parentheses in such an expression will not change its value.

a. Idempotence
c. Algebraically closed

b. Associativity
d. Unital

Chapter 7. Trigonometric Identities, Inverse Functions, and Equations

1. In mathematics, the _____ functions are functions of an angle; they are important when studying triangles and modeling periodic phenomena, among many other applications.
   - a. Law of sines
   - b. Coversine
   - c. Trigonometric
   - d. Gudermannian function

2. In mathematics, _____ are equalities that involve trigonometric functions that are true for every single value of the occurring variables. These identities are useful whenever expressions involving trigonometric functions need to be simplified. An important application is the integration of non-trigonometric functions: a common trick involves first using the substitution rule with a trigonometric function, and then simplifying the resulting integral with a trigonometric identity.
   - a. 120-cell
   - b. 1-center problem
   - c. Trigonometric identities
   - d. 2-3 heap

3. The term _____ or centre is used in various contexts in abstract algebra to denote the set of all those elements that commute with all other elements. More specifically:

   - The _____ of a group G consists of all those elements x in G such that xg = gx for all g in G. This is a normal subgroup of G.
   - The _____ of a ring R is the subset of R consisting of all those elements x of R such that xr = rx for all r in R. The _____ is a commutative subring of R, so R is an algebra over its _____.
   - The _____ of an algebra A consists of all those elements x of A such that xa = ax for all a in A. See also: central simple algebra.
   - The _____ of a Lie algebra L consists of all those elements x in L such that [x,a] = 0 for all a in L. This is an ideal of the Lie algebra L.
   - The _____ of a monoidal category C consists of pairs *a natural isomorphism satisfying certain axioms*.

   - a. Block size
   - b. Disk
   - c. Brute Force
   - d. Center

4. In mathematics, a _____ on a fiber bundle is a device that defines a notion of parallel transport on the bundle; that is, a way to 'connect' or identify fibers over nearby points. If the fiber bundle is a vector bundle, then the notion of parallel transport is required to be linear. Such a _____ is equivalently specified by a covariant derivative, which is an operator that can differentiate sections of that bundle along tangent directions in the base manifold.
   - a. 120-cell
   - b. Connection
   - c. Connectivity
   - d. 1-center problem

5. A _____ is a simple shape of Euclidean geometry consisting of those points in a plane which are at a constant distance, called the radius, from a fixed point, called the center. A _____ with center A is sometimes denoted by the symbol A.

A chord of a _____ is a line segment whose two endpoints lie on the _____.

   - a. Circular segment
   - b. Malfatti circles
   - c. Circumcircle
   - d. Circle

6. An _____ of a real-valued function y = f(x) is a curve which describes the behavior of f as either x or y tends to infinity.

Chapter 7. Trigonometric Identities, Inverse Functions, and Equations

In other words, as one moves along the graph of f(x) in some direction, the distance between it and the _____ eventually becomes smaller than any distance that one may specify.

If a curve A has the curve B as an _____, one says that A is asymptotic to B. Similarly B is asymptotic to A, so A and B are called asymptotic.

   a. Isoperimetric dimension   b. Improper integral
   c. Infinite product   d. Asymptote

7. In geometry and trigonometry, an _____ is the figure formed by two rays sharing a common endpoint, called the vertex of the _____. The magnitude of the _____ is the 'amount of rotation' that separates the two rays, and can be measured by considering the length of circular arc swept out when one ray is rotated about the vertex to coincide with the other. Where there is no possibility of confusion, the term '_____' is used interchangeably for both the geometric configuration itself and for its angular magnitude.

   a. Angle   b. A posteriori
   c. A Mathematical Theory of Communication   d. A chemical equation

8. In mathematics, the _____ is an approach to finding a particular solution to certain inhomogeneous ordinary differential equations and recurrence relations. It is closely related to the annihilator method, but instead of using a particular kind of differential operator in order to find the best possible form of the particular solution, a 'guess' is made as to the appropriate form, which is then tested by differentiating the resulting equation. In this sense, the _____ is less formal but more intuitive than the annihilator method.

   a. Linear differential equation   b. Method of undetermined coefficients
   c. Phase line   d. Differential algebraic equations

9. In mathematics, a function f is _____ of a function g if f whenever A and B are complementary angles. This definition typically applies to trigonometric functions.

   a. Balian-Low theorem   b. Birkhoff interpolation
   c. Boxcar function   d. Cofunction

10. In mathematics, the _____ are functions of an angle. They are important in the study of triangles and modeling periodic phenomena, among many other applications. _____ are commonly defined as ratios of two sides of a right triangle containing the angle, and can equivalently be defined as the lengths of various line segments from a unit circle.

   a. Trigonometric integrals   b. Sine
   c. Law of sines   d. Trigonometric functions

11. An angle smaller than a right angle is called an _____ (less than 90 degrees).

   a. Integral geometry   b. Ultraparallel theorem
   c. Euclidean geometry   d. Acute angle

12. The mathematical concept of a _____ expresses the intuitive idea of deterministic dependence between two quantities, one of which is viewed as primary and the other as secondary. A _____ then is a way to associate a unique output for each input of a specified type, for example, a real number or an element of a given set.

Chapter 7. Trigonometric Identities, Inverse Functions, and Equations

    a. Grill
    b. Coherent
    c. Going up
    d. Function

13. In mathematics, a _____ is a rectangular table of elements, which may be numbers or, more generally, any abstract quantities that can be added and multiplied. Matrices are used to describe linear equations, keep track of the coefficients of linear transformations and to record data that depend on multiple parameters. Matrices are described by the field of _____ theory.
    a. Coherent
    b. Compression
    c. Double counting
    d. Matrix

14. A _____ or sea mile is a unit of length. It corresponds approximately to one minute of latitude along any meridian. It is a non-SI unit used especially by navigators in the shipping and aviation industries.
    a. 120-cell
    b. 2-3 heap
    c. 1-center problem
    d. Nautical mile

15. In mathematics, the _____ of a number n is the number that, when added to n, yields zero. The _____ of n is denoted −n. For example, 7 is −7, because 7 + (−7) = 0, and the _____ of −0.3 is 0.3, because −0.3 + 0.3 = 0.
    a. Arity
    b. Algebraic structure
    c. Additive inverse
    d. Associativity

16. In mathematics, the _____ or cyclometric functions are the so-called inverse functions of the trigonometric functions, though they do not meet the official definition for inverse functions as their domains are subsets of the images of the original functions.
    a. Inverse Trigonometric functions
    b. A Mathematical Theory of Communication
    c. A posteriori
    d. A chemical equation

17. _____ is a branch of mathematics which focuses on the study of matrices. Initially a sub-branch of linear algebra, it has grown to cover subjects related to graph theory, algebra, combinatorics, and statistics as well.

The term matrix was first coined in 1848 by J.J. Sylvester as a name of an array of numbers.

    a. Pairing
    b. Semi-simple operators
    c. Segre classification
    d. Matrix theory

18. An _____ is a function which does the reverse of a given function.
    a. Inverse function
    b. A Mathematical Theory of Communication
    c. Empty set
    d. Empty function

19. A _____ is an abstract model that uses mathematical language to describe the behavior of a system. Eykhoff defined a _____ as 'a representation of the essential aspects of an existing system which presents knowledge of that system in usable form'.
    a. Rata Die
    b. Total least squares
    c. Metaheuristic
    d. Mathematical model

Chapter 7. Trigonometric Identities, Inverse Functions, and Equations

20. In ecology, predation describes a biological interaction where a _____ (an organism that is hunting) feeds on its prey, the organism that is attacked. _____s may or may not kill their prey prior to feeding on them, but the act of predation always results in the death of the prey. The other main category of consumption is detritivory, the consumption of dead organic material (detritus.)

a. 1-center problem
c. Prey
b. Predator
d. 120-cell

21. The _____ is a unit of plane angle, equal to 180/π degrees, or about 57.2958 degrees. It is the standard unit of angular measurement in all areas of mathematics beyond the elementary level.

The _____ is represented by the symbol 'rad' or, more rarely, by the superscript c.

a. 1-center problem
c. 2-3 heap
b. RADIAN
d. 120-cell

22. The _____ fallacy is an informal fallacy. It ascribes cause where none exists. The flaw is failing to account for natural fluctuations.

a. Depth
c. Differential
b. Degrees of freedom
d. Regression

23. The _____ of an angle is the ratio of the length of the opposite side to the length of the hypotenuse. In our case

$$\sin A = \frac{\text{opposite}}{\text{hypotenuse}} = \frac{a}{h}.$$

Note that this ratio does not depend on size of the particular right triangle chosen, as long as it contains the angle A, since all such triangles are similar.

The cosine of an angle is the ratio of the length of the adjacent side to the length of the hypotenuse.

a. Sine
c. Right angle
b. Law of sines
d. Trigonometric functions

24. In statistics, the _____ is the value that occurs the most frequently in a data set or a probability distribution. In some fields, notably education, sample data are often called scores, and the sample _____ is known as the modal score.

Like the statistical mean and the median, the _____ is a way of capturing important information about a random variable or a population in a single quantity.

a. Mode
c. Field
b. Deltoid
d. Function

Chapter 8. Applications of Trigonometry

1. An _____ is a triangle that has one internal angle larger than 90°
   - a. A chemical equation
   - b. Isotomic conjugate
   - c. A Mathematical Theory of Communication
   - d. Obtuse triangle

2. A _____ is one of the basic shapes of geometry: a polygon with three corners or vertices and three sides or edges which are line segments. A _____ with vertices A, B, and C is denoted ABC.

   In Euclidean geometry any three non-collinear points determine a unique _____ and a unique plane.

   - a. Triangle
   - b. Fuhrmann circle
   - c. Kepler triangle
   - d. 1-center problem

3. _____ is a quantity expressing the two-dimensional size of a defined part of a surface, typically a region bounded by a closed curve. The term surface _____ refers to the total _____ of the exposed surface of a 3-dimensional solid, such as the sum of the _____ s of the exposed sides of a polyhedron. _____ is an important invariant in the differential geometry of surfaces.
   - a. A chemical equation
   - b. A Mathematical Theory of Communication
   - c. Area
   - d. A posteriori

4. The _____, in trigonometry, is a statement about any triangle in a plane. Where the sides of the triangle are a, b and c and the angles opposite those sides are A, B and C, then the _____ states equality of the first three quantities below:

$$\underbrace{\frac{a}{\sin A} = \frac{b}{\sin B} = \frac{c}{\sin C}}_{\text{Law of sines}} = 2R$$

   where R is the radius of the triangle's circumcircle. The _____ is also sometimes stated as

$$\frac{\sin A}{a} = \frac{\sin B}{b} = \frac{\sin C}{c}.$$

   This law is useful when computing the remaining sides of a triangle if two angles and a side are known, a common problem in the technique of triangulation.

   - a. Trigonometric functions
   - b. Sine integral
   - c. Trigonometric
   - d. Law of sines

5. The _____ of an angle is the ratio of the length of the opposite side to the length of the hypotenuse. In our case

$$\sin A = \frac{\text{opposite}}{\text{hypotenuse}} = \frac{a}{h}.$$

   Note that this ratio does not depend on size of the particular right triangle chosen, as long as it contains the angle A, since all such triangles are similar.

Chapter 8. Applications of Trigonometry

The cosine of an angle is the ratio of the length of the adjacent side to the length of the hypotenuse.

a. Trigonometric functions
b. Sine
c. Right angle
d. Law of sines

6. In trigonometry, the _____ is a statement about a general triangle which relates the lengths of its sides to the cosine of one of its angles. Using notation as in Fig. 1, the _____ states that

$$c^2 = a^2 + b^2 - 2ab\cos(\gamma),$$

or, equivalently:

$$b^2 = c^2 + a^2 - 2ca\cos(\beta),$$
$$a^2 = b^2 + c^2 - 2bc\cos(\alpha),$$
$$\cos(\gamma) = \frac{a^2 + b^2 - c^2}{2ab}.$$

Note that c is the side opposite of angle γ, and that a and b are the two sides enclosing γ.

a. Trigonometric
b. Law of tangents
c. Law of cosines
d. Trigonometric functions

7. In mathematics and in the sciences, a _____ (plural: _____e, formulæ or _____s) is a concise way of expressing information symbolically (as in a mathematical or chemical _____), or a general relationship between quantities. One of many famous _____e is Albert Einstein's E = mc² (see special relativity

In mathematics, a _____ is a key to solve an equation with variables. For example, the problem of determining the volume of a sphere is one that requires a significant amount of integral calculus to solve.

a. 2-3 heap
b. 1-center problem
c. Formula
d. 120-cell

8. In mathematics, the _____ of a real number is its numerical value without regard to its sign. So, for example, 3 is the _____ of both 3 and −3.

The _____ of a number a is denoted by | a | .

Generalizations of the _____ for real numbers occur in a wide variety of mathematical settings.

a. A chemical equation
b. Area hyperbolic functions
c. A Mathematical Theory of Communication
d. Absolute value

Chapter 8. Applications of Trigonometry

9. In mathematics, the _____s are an extension of the real numbers obtained by adjoining an imaginary unit, denoted i, which satisfies:

$$i^2 = -1.$$

Every _____ can be written in the form a + bi, where a and b are real numbers called the real part and the imaginary part of the _____, respectively.

_____s are a field, and thus have addition, subtraction, multiplication, and division operations. These operations extend the corresponding operations on real numbers, although with a number of additional elegant and useful properties, e.g., negative real numbers can be obtained by squaring _____s.

- a. 1-center problem
- b. Real part
- c. 120-cell
- d. Complex number

10. In mathematics, an _____ is a complex number whose squared value is a real number less than or equal to zero. The imaginary unit, denoted by i or j, is an example of an _____. If y is a real number, then iÂ·y is an _____, because:

$$(i \cdot y)^2 = i^2 \cdot y^2 = -y^2 \leq 0.$$

They were defined in 1572 by Rafael Bombelli.

- a. Imaginary number
- b. A Mathematical Theory of Communication
- c. A posteriori
- d. A chemical equation

11. An _____ of a real-valued function y = f(x) is a curve which describes the behavior of f as either x or y tends to infinity.

In other words, as one moves along the graph of f(x) in some direction, the distance between it and the _____ eventually becomes smaller than any distance that one may specify.

If a curve A has the curve B as an _____, one says that A is asymptotic to B. Similarly B is asymptotic to A, so A and B are called asymptotic.

- a. Isoperimetric dimension
- b. Improper integral
- c. Infinite product
- d. Asymptote

12. In algebra, a _____ of an element in a quadratic extension field of a field K is its image under the unique non-identity automorphism of the extended field that fixes K. If the extension is generated by a square root of an element r of K, then the _____ of $a + b\sqrt{r}$ is $a - b\sqrt{r}$ for $a, b \in K$, and in particular in the case of the field C of complex numbers as an extension of the field R of real numbers, the complex _____ of a + bi is a − bi.

Forming the sum or product of any element of the extension field with its _____ always gives an element of K.

a. Trinomial
c. Relation algebra
b. Real structure
d. Conjugate

13.   In mathematics, a _____ on a fiber bundle is a device that defines a notion of parallel transport on the bundle; that is, a way to 'connect' or identify fibers over nearby points. If the fiber bundle is a vector bundle, then the notion of parallel transport is required to be linear. Such a _____ is equivalently specified by a covariant derivative, which is an operator that can differentiate sections of that bundle along tangent directions in the base manifold.

a. 1-center problem
c. Connectivity
b. 120-cell
d. Connection

14.   A _____ typically refers to a class of handheld calculators that are capable of plotting graphs, solving simultaneous equations, and performing numerous other tasks with variables. Most popular _____s are also programmable, allowing the user to create customized programs, typically for scientific/engineering and education applications. Due to their large displays intended for graphing, they can also accommodate several lines of text and calculations at a time.

a. Bump mapping
c. Support vector machines
b. Genus
d. Graphing calculator

15.   In mathematics, the _____ functions are functions of an angle; they are important when studying triangles and modeling periodic phenomena, among many other applications.

a. Trigonometric
c. Law of sines
b. Gudermannian function
d. Coversine

16.   In elementary algebra, a _____ is a polynomial with two terms: the sum of two monomials. It is the simplest kind of polynomial except for a monomial.

The _____ $a^2 - b^2$ can be factored as the product of two other _____s:

$a^2 - b^2$.

The product of a pair of linear _____s a x + b and c x + d is:

$2 +x + bd$.

A _____ raised to the nth power, represented as

n

can be expanded by means of the _____ theorem or, equivalently, using Pascal's triangle.

a. Cylindrical algebraic decomposition
b. Binomial
c. Real structure
d. Rational root theorem

17. In mathematics, the _____ $\binom{n}{k}$ is the coefficient of the x^k term in the polynomial expansion of the binomial power n.

In combinatorics, $\binom{n}{k}$ is interpreted as the number of k-element subsets of an n-element set, that is the number of ways that k things can be 'chosen' from a set of n things. Hence, $\binom{n}{k}$ is often read as 'n choose k' and called the choose function of n and k.

a. Rule of product
b. Dyson conjecture
c. Binomial coefficient
d. Symbolic combinatorics

18. A _____ is a device for performing mathematical calculations, distinguished from a computer by having a limited problem solving ability and an interface optimized for interactive calculation rather than programming. _____s can be hardware or software, and mechanical or electronic, and are often built into devices such as PDAs or mobile phones.

Modern electronic _____s are generally small, digital, and usually inexpensive.

a. 1-center problem
b. 120-cell
c. 2-3 heap
d. Calculator

19. In mathematics, a _____ is a constant multiplicative factor of a certain object. For example, in the expression $9x^2$, the _____ of x^2 is 9.

The object can be such things as a variable, a vector, a function, etc.

a. Multivariate division algorithm
b. Stability radius
c. Fibonacci polynomials
d. Coefficient

20. _____ is the mathematical operation of scaling one number by another. It is one of the four basic operations in elementary arithmetic.

_____ is defined for whole numbers in terms of repeated addition; for example, 4 multiplied by 3 can be calculated by adding 3 copies of 4 together:

$$4 + 4 + 4 = 12.$$

_____ of rational numbers and real numbers is defined by systematic generalization of this basic idea.

a. The number 0 is even.
b. Least common multiple
c. Highest common factor
d. Multiplication

Chapter 8. Applications of Trigonometry

21. In mathematics, _____ is a property that a binary operation can have. It means that, within an expression containing two or more of the same associative operators in a row, the order that the operations are performed does not matter as long as the sequence of the operands is not changed. That is, rearranging the parentheses in such an expression will not change its value.
   a. Idempotence
   b. Associativity
   c. Unital
   d. Algebraically closed

22. In mathematics, a _____ is a statement that can be proved on the basis of explicitly stated or previously agreed assumptions.
   a. Disjunction introduction
   b. Logical value
   c. Boolean function
   d. Theorem

23. In mathematics, an algebraic group G contains a unique maximal normal solvable subgroup; and this subgroup is closed. Its identity component is called the _____ of G.
   a. Composite
   b. Radical
   c. Barycentric coordinates
   d. Block size

24. A _____ is an expression containing a square root.
   a. Controlled Cryptographic Item
   b. Convolution
   c. Convolution theorem
   d. Radical expression

25. In vascular plants, the _____ is the organ of a plant body that typically lies below the surface of the soil. This is not always the case, however, since a _____ can also be aerial (that is, growing above the ground) or aerating (that is, growing up above the ground or especially above water.) Furthermore, a stem normally occurring below ground is not exceptional either
   a. 120-cell
   b. 2-3 heap
   c. Root
   d. 1-center problem

26. In mathematics, the nth _____ are all the complex numbers which yield 1 when raised to a given power n. It can be shown that they are located on the unit circle of the complex plane and that in that plane they form the vertices of an n-sided regular polygon with one vertex on 1.
   a. 120-cell
   b. Square root of 2
   c. 1-center problem
   d. Roots of unity

27. In mathematics, the _____ system is a two-dimensional coordinate system in which each point on a plane is determined by an angle and a distance. The _____ system is especially useful in situations where the relationship between two points is most easily expressed in terms of angles and distance; in the more familiar Cartesian or rectangular coordinate system, such a relationship can only be found through trigonometric formulation.

As the coordinate system is two-dimensional, each point is determined by two _____s: the radial coordinate and the angular coordinate.

   a. Sir Isaac Newton
   b. Vampire
   c. Sequence alignment
   d. Polar coordinate

Chapter 8. Applications of Trigonometry

28. In complex analysis, a _____ of a meromorphic function is a certain type of singularity that behaves like the singularity $1/z^n$ at z = 0. This means that, in particular, a _____ of the function f

Formally, suppose U is an open subset of the complex plane C, a is an element of U and f : U − {a} → C is a function which is holomorphic over its domain.

a. Harmonic series
b. Decidable
c. Dini
d. Pole

29. In mathematics, the _____ is a two-dimensional coordinate system in which each point on a plane is determined by an angle and a distance. The _____ is especially useful in situations where the relationship between two points is most easily expressed in terms of angles and distance; in the more familiar Cartesian or rectangular coordinate system, such a relationship can only be found through trigonometric formulation.

As the coordinate system is two-dimensional, each point is determined by two polar coordinates: the radial coordinate and the angular coordinate.

a. Sir Isaac Newton
b. Polar Coordinate system
c. Marian Adam Rejewski
d. ROT13

30. _____ is closed curve with one cusp.

In geometry, the _____ is an epicycloid with one cusp.

Rolling circle around another fixed circle produces _____ Conformal mapping from circle to _____

- epicycloid produced as the path of a point on the circumference of a circle as that circle rolls around another fixed circle with the same radius.

- limaçon with one cusp. The cusp is formed when the ratio of a to b in the equation is equal to one.

a. 2-3 heap
b. 120-cell
c. 1-center problem
d. Cardioid

31. In physics and in _____ calculus, a _____ is a concept characterized by a magnitude and a direction. A _____ can be thought of as an arrow in Euclidean space, drawn from an initial point A pointing to a terminal point B.

a. Dominance
b. Vector
c. Constraint
d. Deviation

32. In mathematics, _____ is one of the basic operations defining a vector space in linear algebra. Note that _____ is different from scalar product which is an inner product between two vectors.

More specifically, if K is a field and V is a vector space over K, then _____ is a function from K × V to V.

86   *Chapter 8. Applications of Trigonometry*

a. Non-negative matrix factorization
b. Jordan normal form
c. Frobenius normal form
d. Scalar multiplication

33. In the study of metric spaces in mathematics, there are various notions of two metrics on the same underlying space being 'the same', or _____.

In the following, M will denote a non-empty set and d_1 and d_2 will denote two metrics on M.

The two metrics d_1 and d_2 are said to be topologically _____ if they generate the same topology on M.

a. Equivalent
b. A Mathematical Theory of Communication
c. A posteriori
d. A chemical equation

34. Initial objects are also called _____, and terminal objects are also called final.
a. Direct limit
b. Terminal object
c. Colimit
d. Coterminal

35. In mathematics, a _____ that describes a line D is any vector

where A and B are two distinct points on the line D. If v is a _____ for D, so is kv for any nonzero scalar k; and these are in fact all of the _____s for the line D. Under some definitions, the _____ is required to be a unit vector, in which case each line has exactly two _____s, which are negatives of each other (equal in magnitude, opposite in direction.)

a. Column matrix
b. Reality structure
c. Nullspace
d. Direction Vector

36. In mathematics, an arithmetic progression or _____ is a sequence of numbers such that the difference of any two successive members of the sequence is a constant. For instance, the sequence 3, 5, 7, 9, 11, 13... is an arithmetic progression with common difference 2.
a. Alternating series test
b. Eisenstein series
c. Edgeworth series
d. Arithmetic sequence

37. In geometry, a _____ is a quadrilateral with two sets of parallel sides. The opposite sides of a _____ are of equal length, and the opposite angles of a _____ are congruent. The three-dimensional counterpart of a _____ is a parallelepiped.
a. 2-3 heap
b. 1-center problem
c. 120-cell
d. Parallelogram

38. In mathematics, the simplest form of the _____ belongs to elementary geometry. It states that the sum of the squares of the lengths of the four sides of a parallelogram equals the sum of the squares of the lengths of the two diagonals. With the notation in the diagram on the right, this can be stated as

Chapter 8. Applications of Trigonometry

$$(AB)^2 + (BC)^2 + (CD)^2 + (DA)^2 = (AC)^2 + (BD)^2.$$

In case the parallelogram is a rectangle, the two diagonals are of equal lengths and the statement reduces to the Pythagorean theorem.

a. Homothetic center
c. Square lattice
b. Half-space
d. Parallelogram law

39. In geometry and trigonometry, an _____ is the figure formed by two rays sharing a common endpoint, called the vertex of the _____. The magnitude of the _____ is the 'amount of rotation' that separates the two rays, and can be measured by considering the length of circular arc swept out when one ray is rotated about the vertex to coincide with the other. Where there is no possibility of confusion, the term '_____' is used interchangeably for both the geometric configuration itself and for its angular magnitude.
    a. A Mathematical Theory of Communication
    c. A posteriori
    b. A chemical equation
    d. Angle

40. In algebraic geometry, _____ is a notion of genericity for a set of points, or other geometric objects. It means the general case situation, as opposed to some more special or coincidental cases that are possible. Its precise meaning differs in different settings.
    a. Compactness measure of a shape
    c. Lipschitz domain
    b. Convexity
    d. General position

41. A _____ is a vector which represents the position of an object in space in relation to an arbitrary reference point. The concept applies to two- or three-dimensional space. The term is also used as a means of deriving displacement by the spatial comparison of two or more _____s and are usually 2- or, through hyperspace-based theories, 3-dimensional or N-dimensional if belonging to an N-dimensional Euclidean hyperspace.
    a. Minimum distance
    c. Position Vector
    b. Radius vector
    d. Generalized Morse sequence

42. _____ is a branch of mathematics which focuses on the study of matrices. Initially a sub-branch of linear algebra, it has grown to cover subjects related to graph theory, algebra, combinatorics, and statistics as well.

The term matrix was first coined in 1848 by J.J. Sylvester as a name of an array of numbers.

a. Pairing
c. Segre classification
b. Semi-simple operators
d. Matrix theory

43. In mathematics the _____ of a set which is equipped with the operation of addition is an element which, when added to any element x in the set, yields x. One of the most familiar additive identities is the number 0 from elementary mathematics, but additive identities occur in other mathematical structures where addition is defined, such as in groups and rings.

- The _____ familiar from elementary mathematics is zero, denoted 0. For example,

Chapter 8. Applications of Trigonometry

$5 + 0 = 5 = 0 + 5.$

- In the natural numbers N and all of its supersets, the _____ is 0. Thus for any one of these numbers n,

$n + 0 = n = 0 + n.$

Let N be a set which is closed under the operation of addition, denoted +. An _____ for N is any element e such that for any element n in N,

$e + n = n = n + e.$

a. Algebraically independent
c. Unit ring
b. Unique factorization domain
d. Additive identity

44. In mathematics, the term _____ has several different important meanings:

- An _____ is an equality that remains true regardless of the values of any variables that appear within it, to distinguish it from an equality which is true under more particular conditions. For this, the 'triple bar' symbol ≡ is sometimes used.
- In algebra, an _____ or _____ element of a set S with a binary operation Â· is an element e that, when combined with any element x of S, produces that same x. That is, eÂ·x = xÂ·e = x for all x in S.
    - The _____ function from a set S to itself, often denoted id or id_S, s the function such that i = x for all x in S. This function serves as the _____ element in the set of all functions from S to itself with respect to function composition.
    - In linear algebra, the _____ matrix of size n is the n-by-n square matrix with ones on the main diagonal and zeros elsewhere. This matrix serves as the _____ with respect to matrix multiplication.

A common example of the first meaning is the trigonometric _____

$$\sin^2 \theta + \cos^2 \theta = 1$$

which is true for all real values of θ, as opposed to

$$\cos \theta = 1,$$

which is true only for some values of θ, not all. For example, the latter equation is true when $\theta = 0$, false when $\theta = 2$

The concepts of 'additive _____' and 'multiplicative _____' are central to the Peano axioms. The number 0 is the 'additive _____' for integers, real numbers, and complex numbers. For the real numbers, for all $a \in \mathbb{R}$,

$$0 + a = a,$$

$$a + 0 = a,\text{ and}$$

$$0 + 0 = 0.$$

Similarly, The number 1 is the 'multiplicative _____' for integers, real numbers, and complex numbers.

- a. Action
- b. Intersection
- c. ARIA
- d. Identity

45. In mathematics, a _____ is a rectangular table of elements, which may be numbers or, more generally, any abstract quantities that can be added and multiplied. Matrices are used to describe linear equations, keep track of the coefficients of linear transformations and to record data that depend on multiple parameters. Matrices are described by the field of _____ theory.
    - a. Compression
    - b. Matrix
    - c. Coherent
    - d. Double counting

46. In combinatorial mathematics, a _____ is an un-ordered collection of distinct elements, usually of a prescribed size and taken from a given set. Given such a set S, a _____ of elements of S is just a subset of S, where as always forsets the order of the elements is not taken into account. Also, as always forsets, no elements can be repeated more than once in a _____; this is often referred to as a 'collection without repetition'.
    - a. Fill-in
    - b. Heawood number
    - c. Combination
    - d. Sparsity

47. In mathematics, _____ are a concept central to linear algebra and related fields of mathematics

Suppose that K is a field and V is a vector space over K.

- a. Linear combinations
- b. Polarization
- c. Linear span
- d. Setoid

48. _____ generally conveys two primary meanings. The first is an imprecise sense of harmonious or aesthetically-pleasing proportionality and balance; such that it reflects beauty or perfection. The second meaning is a precise and well-defined concept of balance or 'patterned self-similarity' that can be demonstrated or proved according to the rules of a formal system: by geometry, through physics or otherwise.
    - a. Tessellation
    - b. Symmetry
    - c. Molecular symmetry
    - d. Symmetry breaking

49. In mathematics, the _____ is an operation which takes two vectors over the real numbers R and returns a real-valued scalar quantity. It is the standard inner product of the orthonormal Euclidean space.

The _____ of two vectors a = [a_1, a_2, …, a_n] and b = [b_1, b_2, …, b_n] is defined as:

$$\mathbf{a} \cdot \mathbf{b} = \sum_{i=1}^{n} a_i b_i = a_1 b_1 + a_2 b_2 + \cdots + a_n b_n$$

where Σ denotes summation notation and n is the dimension of the vectors.

a. Dot product
b. Conjugate transpose
c. Matrix determinant lemma
d. Principal axis theorem

50. In mathematics, two vectors are _____ if they are perpendicular. For example, a subway and the street above, although they do not physically intersect, are _____ if they cross at a right angle.

a. Unique factorization domain
b. Additive identity
c. Algebraic structure
d. Orthogonal

Chapter 9. Systems of Equations and Matrices

1. In mathematics, a _____ on a fiber bundle is a device that defines a notion of parallel transport on the bundle; that is, a way to 'connect' or identify fibers over nearby points. If the fiber bundle is a vector bundle, then the notion of parallel transport is required to be linear. Such a _____ is equivalently specified by a covariant derivative, which is an operator that can differentiate sections of that bundle along tangent directions in the base manifold.

    a. 120-cell
    b. Connectivity
    c. 1-center problem
    d. Connection

2. In linear algebra, _____ is an efficient algorithm for solving systems of linear equations, finding the rank of a matrix, and calculating the inverse of an invertible square matrix. _____ is named after German mathematician and scientist Carl Friedrich Gauss.

    Elementary row operations are used to reduce a matrix to row echelon form.

    a. Conjugate gradient method
    b. Cholesky decomposition
    c. Crout matrix decomposition
    d. Gaussian elimination

3. The _____ is a unit of plane angle, equal to 180/π degrees, or about 57.2958 degrees. It is the standard unit of angular measurement in all areas of mathematics beyond the elementary level.

    The _____ is represented by the symbol 'rad' or, more rarely, by the superscript c.

    a. 2-3 heap
    b. 120-cell
    c. 1-center problem
    d. RADIAN

4. An _____ of a real-valued function y = f(x) is a curve which describes the behavior of f as either x or y tends to infinity.

    In other words, as one moves along the graph of f(x) in some direction, the distance between it and the _____ eventually becomes smaller than any distance that one may specify.

    If a curve A has the curve B as an _____, one says that A is asymptotic to B. Similarly B is asymptotic to A, so A and B are called asymptotic.

    a. Infinite product
    b. Asymptote
    c. Isoperimetric dimension
    d. Improper integral

5. In statistics, the _____ is the value that occurs the most frequently in a data set or a probability distribution. In some fields, notably education, sample data are often called scores, and the sample _____ is known as the modal score.

    Like the statistical mean and the median, the _____ is a way of capturing important information about a random variable or a population in a single quantity.

    a. Function
    b. Field
    c. Deltoid
    d. Mode

Chapter 9. Systems of Equations and Matrices

6. In logic, a theory is _____ if it does not contain a contradiction. The lack of contradiction can be defined in either semantic or syntactic terms. The semantic definition states that a theory is _____ if it has a model; this is the sense used in traditional Aristotelian logic, although in contemporary mathematical logic the term satisfiable is used instead.
    a. First-order logic
    b. Second-order logic
    c. Logic
    d. Consistent

7. An _____ is an equation in a system of simultaneous equations which cannot be derived algebraically from the other equations.

    - Linear algebra
    - Indeterminate system

    a. Orthonormal basis
    b. Eigenplane
    c. Antiunitary
    d. Independent equation

8. In the study of metric spaces in mathematics, there are various notions of two metrics on the same underlying space being 'the same', or _____.

    In the following, M will denote a non-empty set and d_1 and d_2 will denote two metrics on M.

    The two metrics d_1 and d_2 are said to be topologically _____ if they generate the same topology on M.

    a. A Mathematical Theory of Communication
    b. Equivalent
    c. A posteriori
    d. A chemical equation

9. _____ is an economic model describing effects on price and quantity in a market. It predicts that in a competitive market, price will function to equalize the quantity demanded by consumers, and the quantity supplied by producers, resulting in an economic equilibrium of price and quantity. The model incorporates other factors changing equilibrium as a shift of demand and/or supply.
    a. 1-center problem
    b. Marginal rate of substitution
    c. Cross price elasticity of demand
    d. Supply and demand

10. In mathematics, the point $\tilde{\mathbf{x}} \in \mathbb{R}^n$ is an _____ for the differential equation

$$\frac{d\mathbf{x}}{dt} = \mathbf{f}(t, \mathbf{x})$$

if $\mathbf{f}(t, \tilde{\mathbf{x}}) = 0$ for all t.

Similarly, the point $\tilde{\mathbf{x}} \in \mathbb{R}^n$ is an _____ for the difference equation

$$\mathbf{x}_{k+1} = \mathbf{f}(k, \mathbf{x}_k)$$

if $\mathbf{f}(k, \tilde{\mathbf{x}}) = \tilde{\mathbf{x}}$ for $k = 0, 1, 2, \ldots$.

Equilibria can be classified by looking at the signs of the eigenvalues of the linearization of the equations about the equilibria.

a. Algorithm design
c. Unitary transformation
b. Uniform algebra
d. Equilibrium point

11. In economics, specifically cost accounting, the _____ is the point at which cost or expenses and revenue are equal: there is no net loss or gain, and one has 'broken even'. Therefore has not made a profit or a loss.

In the linear Cost-Volume-Profit Analysis model, the _____ can be directly computed in terms of Total Revenue and Total Costs as:

$$\begin{aligned} TR &= TC \\ P \times X &= TFC + V \times X \\ P \times X - V \times X &= TFC \\ (P - V) \times X &= TFC \\ X &= \frac{TFC}{P - V} \end{aligned}$$

where:

- TFC is Total Fixed Costs,
- P is Unit Sale Price, and
- V is Unit Variable Cost.

The _____ can alternatively be computed as the point where Contribution equals Fixed Costs.

The quantity $(P - V)$ is of interest in its own right, and is called the Unit Contribution Margin: it is the marginal profit per unit, or alternatively the portion of each sale that contributes to Fixed Costs. Thus the _____ can be more simply computed as the point where Total Contribution = Total Fixed Cost:

$$\begin{aligned} \text{Total Contribution} &= \text{Total Fixed Costs} \\ \text{Unit Contribution} \times \text{Number of Units} &= \text{Total Fixed Costs} \\ \text{Number of Units} &= \frac{\text{Total Fixed Costs}}{\text{Unit Contribution}} \end{aligned}$$

In currency units to reach break-even, one can use the above calculation and multiply by Price, or equivalently use the

$$\text{Break-even(in Sales)} = \frac{\text{Fixed Costs}}{C/P}.$$

Contribution Margin Ratio to compute it as:

R=C Where R is revenue generated C is cost incurred.

a. Small numbers game
c. 120-cell
b. Break-even point
d. 1-center problem

12. A _____ is an algebraic equation in which each term is either a constant or the product of a constant and a single variable. _____s can have one, two, three or more variables.

_____s occur with great regularity in applied mathematics.

a. Linear equation
c. Quartic equation
b. Quadratic equation
d. Difference of two squares

13. In quantum field theory and statistical mechanics in the thermodynamic limit, a system with a global symmetry can have more than one phase. For parameters where the symmetry is spontaneously broken, the system is said to be _____. When the global symmetry is unbroken the system is disordered.

a. Isoenthalpic-isobaric ensemble
c. Einstein relation
b. Ursell function
d. Ordered

14. A _____ is an abstract model that uses mathematical language to describe the behavior of a system. Eykhoff defined a _____ as 'a representation of the essential aspects of an existing system which presents knowledge of that system in usable form'.

a. Metaheuristic
c. Mathematical model
b. Rata Die
d. Total least squares

15. In ecology, predation describes a biological interaction where a _____ (an organism that is hunting) feeds on its prey, the organism that is attacked. _____s may or may not kill their prey prior to feeding on them, but the act of predation always results in the death of the prey. The other main category of consumption is detritivory, the consumption of dead organic material (detritus.)

a. 1-center problem
c. Prey
b. 120-cell
d. Predator

16. In linear algebra, the _____ of a matrix is obtained by changing a matrix in some way.

Given the matrices A and B, where:

$$A = \begin{bmatrix} 1 & 3 & 2 \\ 2 & 0 & 1 \\ 5 & 2 & 2 \end{bmatrix}, \quad B = \begin{bmatrix} 4 \\ 3 \\ 1 \end{bmatrix}$$

Then, the _____ is written as:

$$(A|B) = \begin{bmatrix} 1 & 3 & 2 & 4 \\ 2 & 0 & 1 & 3 \\ 5 & 2 & 2 & 1 \end{bmatrix}$$

This is useful when solving systems of linear equations or the _____ may also be used to find the inverse of a matrix by combining it with the identity matrix.

Chapter 9. Systems of Equations and Matrices

Let C be a square 2×2 matrix where $C = \begin{bmatrix} 1 & 3 \\ -5 & 0 \end{bmatrix}$

To find the inverse of C we create where I is the 2×2 identity matrix.

a. Unimodular polynomial matrix
c. Alternating sign matrix
b. Augmented matrix
d. Eigendecomposition

17. In mathematics, a _____ is a constant multiplicative factor of a certain object. For example, in the expression $9x^2$, the _____ of x^2 is 9.

The object can be such things as a variable, a vector, a function, etc.

a. Coefficient
c. Stability radius
b. Multivariate division algorithm
d. Fibonacci polynomials

18. _____ is a branch of mathematics which focuses on the study of matrices. Initially a sub-branch of linear algebra, it has grown to cover subjects related to graph theory, algebra, combinatorics, and statistics as well.

The term matrix was first coined in 1848 by J.J. Sylvester as a name of an array of numbers.

a. Segre classification
c. Semi-simple operators
b. Pairing
d. Matrix theory

19. In mathematics, an _____ in the sense of ring theory is a subring $\mathcal{O}$ of a ring R that satisfies the conditions

1. R is a ring which is a finite-dimensional algebra over the rational number field $\mathbb{Q}$
2. $\mathcal{O}$ spans R over $\mathbb{Q}$, so that $\mathbb{Q}\mathcal{O} = R$, and
3. $\mathcal{O}$ is a lattice in R.

The third condition can be stated more accurately, in terms of the extension of scalars of R to the real numbers, embedding R in a real vector space. In less formal terms, additively $\mathcal{O}$ should be a free abelian group generated by a basis for R over $\mathbb{Q}$.

The leading example is the case where R is a number field K and $\mathcal{O}$ is its ring of integers. In algebraic number theory there are examples for any K other than the rational field of proper subrings of the ring of integers that are also _____ s.

a. Algebraic
c. Annihilator
b. Efficiency
d. Order

20. The _____ fallacy is an informal fallacy. It ascribes cause where none exists. The flaw is failing to account for natural fluctuations.

a. Depth
b. Degrees of freedom
c. Differential
d. Regression

21. In mathematics, a _____ is a rectangular table of elements, which may be numbers or, more generally, any abstract quantities that can be added and multiplied. Matrices are used to describe linear equations, keep track of the coefficients of linear transformations and to record data that depend on multiple parameters. Matrices are described by the field of _____ theory.

   a. Compression
   b. Coherent
   c. Matrix
   d. Double counting

22. In linear algebra a matrix is in _____ if

- All nonzero rows are above any rows of all zeroes, and
- The leading coefficient of a row is always strictly to the right of the leading coefficient of the row above it.

This is the definition used in this article, but some texts add a third condition:

- The leading coefficient of each nonzero row is one.

A matrix is in reduced row echelon form if it satisfies the above three conditions, and if, in addition

- Every leading coefficient is the only nonzero entry in its column.

The first non-zero entry in each row is called a pivot.

This matrix is in reduced row echelon form:

$$\begin{bmatrix} 0 & 1 & 4 & 0 & 0 \\ 0 & 0 & 0 & 1 & 0 \\ 0 & 0 & 0 & 0 & 1 \\ 0 & 0 & 0 & 0 & 0 \end{bmatrix}.$$

The following matrix is also in row echelon form, but not in reduced row form:

$$\begin{bmatrix} 1 & 1 & 1 & 1 \\ 0 & 9 & 0 & 2 \\ 0 & 0 & 0 & 3 \end{bmatrix}.$$

However, this matrix is not in row echelon form, as the leading coefficient of row 3 is not strictly to the right of the leading coefficient of row 2.

$$\begin{bmatrix} 1 & 2 & 3 & 4 \\ 0 & 3 & 7 & 2 \\ 0 & 2 & 0 & 0 \end{bmatrix}$$

Every non-zero matrix can be reduced to an infinite number of echelon forms via elementary matrix transformations.

a. Folded spectrum method
c. Circulant matrix
b. Power iteration
d. Row-echelon form

23. In linear algebra, _____ is a version of Gaussian elimination that puts zeros both above and below each pivot element as it goes from the top row of the given matrix to the bottom. In other words, _____ brings a matrix to reduced row echelon form, whereas Gaussian elimination takes it only as far as row echelon form. Every matrix has a reduced row echelon form, and this algorithm is guaranteed to produce it.

a. Spheroidal wave functions
c. Lax equivalence theorem
b. Gauss-Jordan elimination
d. Conservation form

24. In mathematics, _____ is a property that a binary operation can have. It means that, within an expression containing two or more of the same associative operators in a row, the order that the operations are performed does not matter as long as the sequence of the operands is not changed. That is, rearranging the parentheses in such an expression will not change its value.

a. Idempotence
c. Algebraically closed
b. Associativity
d. Unital

25. In elementary algebra, a _____ is a polynomial with two terms: the sum of two monomials. It is the simplest kind of polynomial except for a monomial.

The _____ $a^2 - b^2$ can be factored as the product of two other _____s:

$a^2 - b^2$.

The product of a pair of linear _____s a x + b and c x + d is:

2 +x + bd.

A _____ raised to the nth power, represented as

n

can be expanded by means of the _____ theorem or, equivalently, using Pascal's triangle.

a. Real structure
c. Rational root theorem
b. Cylindrical algebraic decomposition
d. Binomial

26. In mathematics, the _____ $\binom{n}{k}$ is the coefficient of the x^k term in the polynomial expansion of the binomial power ^{n}.

In combinatorics, $\binom{n}{k}$ is interpreted as the number of k-element subsets of an n-element set, that is the number of ways that k things can be 'chosen' from a set of n things. Hence, $\binom{n}{k}$ is often read as 'n choose k' and called the choose function of n and k.

a. Rule of product
b. Symbolic combinatorics
c. Dyson conjecture
d. Binomial coefficient

27. In mathematics, the _____s are an extension of the real numbers obtained by adjoining an imaginary unit, denoted i, which satisfies:

$$i^2 = -1.$$

Every _____ can be written in the form a + bi, where a and b are real numbers called the real part and the imaginary part of the _____, respectively.

_____s are a field, and thus have addition, subtraction, multiplication, and division operations. These operations extend the corresponding operations on real numbers, although with a number of additional elegant and useful properties, e.g., negative real numbers can be obtained by squaring _____s.

a. 120-cell
b. Complex number
c. Real part
d. 1-center problem

28. In mathematics the _____ of a set which is equipped with the operation of addition is an element which, when added to any element x in the set, yields x. One of the most familiar additive identities is the number 0 from elementary mathematics, but additive identities occur in other mathematical structures where addition is defined, such as in groups and rings.

- The _____ familiar from elementary mathematics is zero, denoted 0. For example,

  5 + 0 = 5 = 0 + 5.

- In the natural numbers N and all of its supersets, the _____ is 0. Thus for any one of these numbers n,

  n + 0 = n = 0 + n.

Let N be a set which is closed under the operation of addition, denoted +. An _____ for N is any element e such that for any element n in N,

e + n = n = n + e.

a. Additive identity
b. Algebraically independent
c. Unit ring
d. Unique factorization domain

29. In mathematics, the _____ of a number n is the number that, when added to n, yields zero. The _____ of n is denoted −n. For example, 7 is −7, because 7 + (−7) = 0, and the _____ of −0.3 is 0.3, because −0.3 + 0.3 = 0.
a. Associativity
b. Algebraic structure
c. Arity
d. Additive inverse

Chapter 9. Systems of Equations and Matrices

30. _____ is the mathematical operation of scaling one number by another. It is one of the four basic operations in elementary arithmetic.

_____ is defined for whole numbers in terms of repeated addition; for example, 4 multiplied by 3 can be calculated by adding 3 copies of 4 together:

$$4 + 4 + 4 = 12.$$

_____ of rational numbers and real numbers is defined by systematic generalization of this basic idea.

a. The number 0 is even.
b. Least common multiple
c. Highest common factor
d. Multiplication

31. In mathematics, _____ is one of the basic operations defining a vector space in linear algebra. Note that _____ is different from scalar product which is an inner product between two vectors.

More specifically, if K is a field and V is a vector space over K, then _____ is a function from K × V to V.

a. Scalar multiplication
b. Jordan normal form
c. Non-negative matrix factorization
d. Frobenius normal form

32. The mathematical concept of a _____ expresses the intuitive idea of deterministic dependence between two quantities, one of which is viewed as primary and the other as secondary. A _____ then is a way to associate a unique output for each input of a specified type, for example, a real number or an element of a given set.
a. Grill
b. Function
c. Going up
d. Coherent

33. In mathematics, the term _____ has several different important meanings:

- An _____ is an equality that remains true regardless of the values of any variables that appear within it, to distinguish it from an equality which is true under more particular conditions. For this, the 'triple bar' symbol ≡ is sometimes used.
- In algebra, an _____ or _____ element of a set S with a binary operation Â· is an element e that, when combined with any element x of S, produces that same x. That is, eÂ·x = xÂ·e = x for all x in S.
    - The _____ function from a set S to itself, often denoted id or id_S, s the function such that i = x for all x in S. This function serves as the _____ element in the set of all functions from S to itself with respect to function composition.
    - In linear algebra, the _____ matrix of size n is the n-by-n square matrix with ones on the main diagonal and zeros elsewhere. This matrix serves as the _____ with respect to matrix multiplication.

A common example of the first meaning is the trigonometric _____

$$\sin^2 \theta + \cos^2 \theta = 1$$

which is true for all real values of θ, as opposed to

$$\cos\theta = 1,$$

which is true only for some values of θ, not all. For example, the latter equation is true when $\theta = 0$, false when $\theta = 2$

The concepts of 'additive _____' and 'multiplicative _____' are central to the Peano axioms. The number 0 is the 'additive _____' for integers, real numbers, and complex numbers. For the real numbers, for all $a \in \mathbb{R}$,

$$0 + a = a,$$

$$a + 0 = a, \text{ and}$$

$$0 + 0 = 0.$$

Similarly, The number 1 is the 'multiplicative _____' for integers, real numbers, and complex numbers.

a. Intersection
c. Action
b. ARIA
d. Identity

34. In mathematics, and in particular in abstract algebra, distributivity is a property of binary operations that generalises the _____ law from elementary algebra.
   a. General linear group
   c. Closure with a twist
   b. Permutation
   d. Distributive

35. In mathematics, _____ is the operation of adding two matrices by adding the corresponding entries together. However, there is another operation which could also be considered as a kind of addition for matrices.

The usual _____ is defined for two matrices of the same dimensions.

   a. Jordan normal form
   c. Spectral theory
   b. Standard basis
   d. Matrix addition

36. In linear algebra, a column vector or _____ is an m × 1 matrix, i.e. a matrix consisting of a single column of m elements.

$$\mathbf{x} = \begin{bmatrix} x_1 \\ x_2 \\ \vdots \\ x_m \end{bmatrix}$$

The transpose of a column vector is a row vector and vice versa.

The set of all column vectors forms a vector space which is the dual space to the set of all row vectors.

a. Cayley-Hamilton theorem
b. Split-complex number
c. Column matrix
d. Spread of a matrix

37. In linear algebra, a row vector or _____ is a 1 × n matrix, that is, a matrix consisting of a single row:

$$\mathbf{x} = \begin{bmatrix} x_1 & x_2 & \ldots & x_m \end{bmatrix}.$$

The transpose of a row vector is a column vector:

$$\begin{bmatrix} x_1 \\ x_2 \\ \vdots \\ x_m \end{bmatrix} = \begin{bmatrix} x_1 & x_2 & \ldots & x_m \end{bmatrix}^{\mathrm{T}}.$$

The set of all row vectors forms a vector space which is the dual space to the set of all column vectors.

Row vectors are sometimes written using the following non-standard notation:

$$\mathbf{x} = \begin{bmatrix} x_1, x_2, \ldots, x_m \end{bmatrix}.$$

- Matrix multiplication involves the action of multiplying each row vector of one matrix by each column vector of another matrix.

- The dot product of two vectors a and b is equivalent to multiplying the row vector representation of a by the column vector representation of b:

$$\mathbf{a} \cdot \mathbf{b} = \begin{bmatrix} a_1 & a_2 & a_3 \end{bmatrix} \begin{bmatrix} b_1 \\ b_2 \\ b_3 \end{bmatrix}.$$

a. Woodbury matrix identity
b. Gram-Schmidt process
c. Dual vector space
d. Row matrix

38. In mathematics, _____ is the operation of multiplying a matrix with either a scalar or another matrix

This is the most often used and most important way to multiply matrices.

a. Logarithmic norm
b. Matrix calculus
c. Matrix multiplication
d. Jordan matrix

39. In linear algebra, the _____ or unit matrix of size n is the n-by-n square matrix with ones on the main diagonal and zeros elsewhere. It is denoted by I_n, or simply by I if the size is immaterial or can be trivially determined by the context. (In some fields, such as quantum mechanics, the _____ is denoted by a boldface one, 1; otherwise it is identical to I.)

a. Unital
b. Associativity
c. Arity
d. Identity matrix

40. In mathematics, a _____ for a number x, denoted by $1/x$ or x^{-1}, is a number which when multiplied by x yields the multiplicative identity, 1. The _____ of x is also called the reciprocal of x. The _____ of a fraction p/q is q/p.
   a. Golden function
   b. Multiplicative inverse
   c. Double exponential
   d. Hyperbolic function

41. If $A_1, A_2, ..., A_n$ are _____ square matrices over a field, then

$$(A_1 A_2 \cdots A_n)^{-1} = A_n^{-1} A_{n-1}^{-1} \cdots A_1^{-1}.$$

It becomes evident why this is the case if one attempts to find an inverse for the product of the A_is from first principles, that is, that we wish to determine B such that

$$(A_1 A_2 \cdots A_n)B = I$$

where B is the inverse matrix of the product. To remove A_1 from the product, we can then write

$$A_1^{-1}(A_1 A_2 \cdots A_n)B = A_1^{-1} I$$

which would reduce the equation to

$$(A_2 A_3 \cdots A_n)B = A_1^{-1} I.$$

Likewise, then, from

$$A_2^{-1}(A_2 A_3 \cdots A_n)B = A_2^{-1} A_1^{-1} I$$

which simplifies to

$$(A_3 A_4 \cdots A_n)B = A_2^{-1} A_1^{-1} I.$$

If one repeat the process up to A_n, the equation becomes

$$B = A_n^{-1} A_{n-1}^{-1} \cdots A_2^{-1} A_1^{-1} I$$

$$B = A_n^{-1} A_{n-1}^{-1} \cdots A_2^{-1} A_1^{-1}$$

but B is the inverse matrix, i.e. $\mathbf{B} = (\mathbf{A}_1 \mathbf{A}_2 \cdots \mathbf{A}_n)^{-1}$ so the property is established.

Over the field of real numbers, the set of singular n-by-n matrices, considered as a subset of $R^{n \times n}$, is a null set, i.e., has Lebesgue measure zero.

a. Projection-valued measure
b. Matrix pencil
c. Nonsingular
d. Jordan normal form

42. In algebra, a _____ is a function depending on n that associates a scalar, de, to every n×n square matrix A. The fundamental geometric meaning of a _____ is as the scale factor for measure when A is regarded as a linear transformation. _____s are important both in calculus, where they enter the substitution rule for several variables, and in multilinear algebra.

a. Pfaffian
b. Functional determinant
c. 1-center problem
d. Determinant

43. In linear algebra, a _____ of a matrix A is the determinant of some smaller square matrix, cut down from A by removing one or more of its rows or columns.

_____s obtained by removing just one row and one column from square matrices are required for calculating matrix cofactors, which in turn are useful for computing both the determinant and inverse of square matrices.

Let A be an m × n matrix and k an integer with 0 < k ≤ m, and k ≤ n.

a. Chiral
b. Block size
c. Minor
d. Homogeneity

44. _____ is either of the two parts into which a plane divides the three-dimensional space. More generally, a _____ is either of the two parts into which a hyperplane divides an affine space.

a. Pendent
b. Simple polytope
c. Parallelogram law
d. Half-space

45. In mathematics, an _____ is a statement about the relative size or order of two objects, or about whether they are the same or not

- The notation a < b means that a is less than b.
- The notation a > b means that a is greater than b.
- The notation a ≠ b means that a is not equal to b, but does not say that one is bigger than the other or even that they can be compared in size.

In all these cases, a is not equal to b, hence, '_____'.

These relations are known as strict _____

- The notation a ≤ b means that a is less than or equal to b;
- The notation a ≥ b means that a is greater than or equal to b;

An additional use of the notation is to show that one quantity is much greater than another, normally by several orders of magnitude.

- The notation a << b means that a is much less than b.
- The notation a >> b means that a is much greater than b.

If the sense of the _____ is the same for all values of the variables for which its members are defined, then the _____ is called an 'absolute' or 'unconditional' _____. If the sense of an _____ holds only for certain values of the variables involved, but is reversed or destroyed for other values of the variables, it is called a conditional _____.

An _____ may appear unsolvable because it only states whether a number is larger or smaller than another number; but it is possible to apply the same operations for equalities to inequalities. For example, to find x for the _____ 10x > 23 one would divide 23 by 10.

a. A posteriori
b. A Mathematical Theory of Communication
c. A chemical equation
d. Inequality

46. In mathematics, an _____ or member of a set is any one of the distinct objects that make up that set.

Writing A = {1,2,3,4}, means that the _____s of the set A are the numbers 1, 2, 3 and 4. Groups of _____s of A, for example {1,2}, are subsets of A.

a. Universal code
b. Ideal
c. Order
d. Element

47. In mathematics, a _____ is a condition that a solution to an optimization problem must satisfy. There are two types of _____s: equality _____s and inequality _____s. The set of solutions that satisfy all _____s is called the feasible set.

a. Decidable
b. Foci
c. Concurrent
d. Constraint

48. In mathematics, _____ is a technique for optimization of a linear objective function, subject to linear equality and linear inequality constraints. Informally, _____ determines the way to achieve the best outcome in a given mathematical model given some list of requirements represented as linear equations.

More formally, given a polytope, and a real-valued affine function

$$f(x_1, x_2, \ldots, x_n) = c_1 x_1 + c_2 x_2 + \cdots + c_n x_n + d$$

defined on this polytope, a _____ method will find a point in the polytope where this function has the smallest value.

a. Lin-Kernighan
b. Descent direction
c. Linear programming relaxation
d. Linear programming

49. An _____ is a tree data structure in which each internal node has up to eight children. _____s are most often used to partition a three dimensional space by recursively subdividing it into eight octants. _____s are the three-dimensional analog of quadtrees.

a. Interval tree
b. Adaptive k-d tree
c. Octree
d. External node

50. In mathematics, the adjective _____ means that an object cannot be expressed as a product of at least two non-trivial factors in a given set.

For any field F, the ring of polynomials with coefficients in F is denoted by F[x].

a. Integer-valued polynomial
b. Irreducible
c. Euler-Worpitzky-Chen polynomials
d. Ehrhart polynomial

51. In algebra, the _____ decomposition or _____ expansion is used to reduce the degree of either the numerator or the denominator of a rational function. The outcome of _____ expansion expresses that function as a sum of fractions, where:

- the denominator of each term is a power of an irreducible polynomial and
- the numerator is a polynomial of smaller degree than that irreducible polynomial.

See _____s in integration for an account of their use in finding antiderivatives. They are also used in calculating the inverse of transforms; such as the Laplace transform, or the Z-transform.

The basic idea behind _____s is to work backwards to separate a function.

a. Real structure
b. Continuant
c. Concept algebra
d. Partial fraction

Chapter 10. Conic Sections

1. A _____ is a simple shape of Euclidean geometry consisting of those points in a plane which are at a constant distance, called the radius, from a fixed point, called the center. A _____ with center A is sometimes denoted by the symbol A.

A chord of a _____ is a line segment whose two endpoints lie on the _____.

   a. Circumcircle
   b. Circle
   c. Malfatti circles
   d. Circular segment

2. In mathematics, a _____ is a curve obtained by intersecting a cone with a plane. A _____ is therefore a restriction of a quadric surface to the plane. The _____s were named and studied as long ago as 200 BC, when Apollonius of Perga undertook a systematic study of their properties.

   a. Directrix
   b. Conic section
   c. Dandelin sphere
   d. Parabola

3. The latus rectum (2l) is the chord parallel to the _____ and passing through the focus (or one of the two foci.)

The semi-latus rectum (l) is half the latus rectum.

The focal parameter (p) is the distance from the focus (or one of the two foci) to the _____.

   a. Parabola
   b. Directrix
   c. Matrix representation of conic sections
   d. Conic section

4. In mathematics an _____ , a 'falling short') is a conic section, the locus of points in a plane such that the sum of the distances to two fixed points is equal to a given constant. The two fixed points are then called foci.

Another way is to define it as the path traced out by a point whose distance from a focus maintains a constant ratio less than one with its distance from a straight line not passing through the focus, called the directrix.

   a. A chemical equation
   b. Ellipse
   c. A Mathematical Theory of Communication
   d. A posteriori

5. In mathematics, the _____ is a conic section, the intersection of a right circular conical surface and a plane parallel to a generating straight line of that surface. Given a point and a line that lie in a plane, the locus of points in that plane that are equidistant to them is a _____.

A particular case arises when the plane is tangent to the conical surface of a circle.

   a. Dandelin sphere
   b. Matrix representation of conic sections
   c. Directrix
   d. Parabola

6. _____ generally conveys two primary meanings. The first is an imprecise sense of harmonious or aesthetically-pleasing proportionality and balance; such that it reflects beauty or perfection. The second meaning is a precise and well-defined concept of balance or 'patterned self-similarity' that can be demonstrated or proved according to the rules of a formal system: by geometry, through physics or otherwise.

a. Symmetry
b. Symmetry breaking
c. Molecular symmetry
d. Tessellation

7. In geometry, a _____ is a special kind of point, usually a corner of a polygon, polyhedron, or higher dimensional polytope. In the geometry of curves a _____ is a point of where the first derivative of curvature is zero. In graph theory, a _____ is the fundamental unit out of which graphs are formed
   a. Vertex
   b. Dini
   c. Duality
   d. Crib

8. In geometry and trigonometry, an _____ is the figure formed by two rays sharing a common endpoint, called the vertex of the _____. The magnitude of the _____ is the 'amount of rotation' that separates the two rays, and can be measured by considering the length of circular arc swept out when one ray is rotated about the vertex to coincide with the other. Where there is no possibility of confusion, the term '_____' is used interchangeably for both the geometric configuration itself and for its angular magnitude.
   a. A Mathematical Theory of Communication
   b. A posteriori
   c. Angle
   d. A chemical equation

9. An _____ of a real-valued function y = f(x) is a curve which describes the behavior of f as either x or y tends to infinity.

In other words, as one moves along the graph of f(x) in some direction, the distance between it and the _____ eventually becomes smaller than any distance that one may specify.

If a curve A has the curve B as an _____, one says that A is asymptotic to B. Similarly B is asymptotic to A, so A and B are called asymptotic.

   a. Isoperimetric dimension
   b. Improper integral
   c. Infinite product
   d. Asymptote

10. A _____ is a three-dimensional geometric shape that tapers smoothly from a flat, round base to a point called the apex or vertex. More precisely, it is the solid figure bounded by a plane base and the surface formed by the locus of all straight line segments joining the apex to the perimeter of the base. The term '_____' sometimes refers just to the surface of this solid figure, or just to the lateral surface.
    a. Gravity waves
    b. Cone
    c. Blocking
    d. Characteristic

11. In algebra, a _____ of an element in a quadratic extension field of a field K is its image under the unique non-identity automorphism of the extended field that fixes K. If the extension is generated by a square root of an element r of K, then the _____ of $a + b\sqrt{r}$ is $a - b\sqrt{r}$ for $a, b \in K$, and in particular in the case of the field C of complex numbers as an extension of the field R of real numbers, the complex _____ of a + bi is a − bi.

Forming the sum or product of any element of the extension field with its _____ always gives an element of K.

a. Relation algebra
c. Trinomial

b. Real structure
d. Conjugate

12. _____, also sometimes known as standard form or as exponential notation, is a way of writing numbers that accommodates values too large or small to be conveniently written in standard decimal notation. _____ has a number of useful properties and is often favored by scientists, mathematicians and engineers, who work with such numbers.

In _____, numbers are written in the form:

$$a \times 10^b$$

a. Radix point
c. Leading zero

b. Scientific notation
d. 1-center problem

13. In mathematics, a _____ on a fiber bundle is a device that defines a notion of parallel transport on the bundle; that is, a way to 'connect' or identify fibers over nearby points. If the fiber bundle is a vector bundle, then the notion of parallel transport is required to be linear. Such a _____ is equivalently specified by a covariant derivative, which is an operator that can differentiate sections of that bundle along tangent directions in the base manifold.

a. Connectivity
c. 1-center problem

b. 120-cell
d. Connection

14. In physics and geometry, the _____ is the theoretical shape of a hanging flexible chain or cable when supported at its ends and acted upon by a uniform gravitational force and in equilibrium. The curve has a U shape that is similar in appearance to the parabola, though it is a different curve.

The word _____ is derived from the Latin word catena, which means 'chain'.

a. 120-cell
c. 2-3 heap

b. 1-center problem
d. Catenary

15. A _____ is a software program that facilitates symbolic mathematics. The core functionality of a CAS is manipulation of mathematical expressions in symbolic form.

Chapter 10. Conic Sections

The symbolic manipulations supported typically include

- simplification to the smallest possible expression or some standard form, including automatic simplification with assumptions and simplification with constraints
- substitution of symbolic, functors or numeric values for expressions
- change of form of expressions: expanding products and powers, partial and full factorization, rewriting as partial fractions, constraint satisfaction, rewriting trigonometric functions as exponentials, etc.
- partial and total differentiation
- symbolic constrained and unconstrained global optimization
- solution of linear and some non-linear equations over various domains
- solution of some differential and difference equations
- taking some limits
- some indefinite and definite integration, including multidimensional integrals
- integral transforms
- arbitrary-precision numeric operations
- Series operations such as expansion, summation and products
- matrix operations including products, inverses, etc.
- display of mathematical expressions in two-dimensional mathematical form, often using typesetting systems similar to TeX
- add-ons for use in applied mathematics such as physics packages for physical computation
- plotting graphs and parametric plots of functions in two and three dimensions, and animating them
- APIs for linking it on an external program such as a database, or using in a programming language to use the _____
- drawing charts and diagrams
- string manipulation such as matching and searching
- statistical computation
- Theorem proving and verification
- graphic production and editing such as CGI and signal processing as image processing
- sound synthesis

Many also include a programming language, allowing users to implement their own algorithms.

Some _____s focus on a specific area of application; these are typically developed in academia and are free.

a. 1-center problem
c. 2-3 heap
b. 120-cell
d. Computer algebra system

16. The term _____ or centre is used in various contexts in abstract algebra to denote the set of all those elements that commute with all other elements. More specifically:

- The _____ of a group G consists of all those elements x in G such that xg = gx for all g in G. This is a normal subgroup of G.
- The _____ of a ring R is the subset of R consisting of all those elements x of R such that xr = rx for all r in R. The _____ is a commutative subring of R, so R is an algebra over its _____.
- The _____ of an algebra A consists of all those elements x of A such that xa = ax for all a in A. See also: central simple algebra.
- The _____ of a Lie algebra L consists of all those elements x in L such that [x,a] = 0 for all a in L. This is an ideal of the Lie algebra L.
- The _____ of a monoidal category C consists of pairs *a natural isomorphism satisfying certain axioms*.

a. Block size
b. Disk
c. Brute Force
d. Center

17. A _____ typically refers to a class of handheld calculators that are capable of plotting graphs, solving simultaneous equations, and performing numerous other tasks with variables. Most popular _____s are also programmable, allowing the user to create customized programs, typically for scientific/engineering and education applications. Due to their large displays intended for graphing, they can also accommodate several lines of text and calculations at a time.

a. Genus
b. Support vector machines
c. Bump mapping
d. Graphing calculator

18. In mathematics, the _____ of a real number is its numerical value without regard to its sign. So, for example, 3 is the _____ of both 3 and −3.

The _____ of a number a is denoted by $|a|$.

Generalizations of the _____ for real numbers occur in a wide variety of mathematical settings.

a. A chemical equation
b. Area hyperbolic functions
c. A Mathematical Theory of Communication
d. Absolute value

19. A _____ is a device for performing mathematical calculations, distinguished from a computer by having a limited problem solving ability and an interface optimized for interactive calculation rather than programming. _____s can be hardware or software, and mechanical or electronic, and are often built into devices such as PDAs or mobile phones.

Modern electronic _____s are generally small, digital, and usually inexpensive.

a. Calculator
b. 1-center problem
c. 120-cell
d. 2-3 heap

20. In geometry, the semi-_____ (also semimajor axis) is used to describe the dimensions of ellipses and hyperbolae.

The _____ of an ellipse is its longest diameter, a line that runs through the centre and both foci, its ends being at the widest points of the shape. The semi-_____ is one half of the _____, and thus runs from the centre, through a focus, and to the edge of the ellipse.

a. Lagrangian points
b. Lagrange points
c. Semi-major axis
d. Major axis

21. In linear algebra, a _____ of a matrix A is the determinant of some smaller square matrix, cut down from A by removing one or more of its rows or columns.

_____s obtained by removing just one row and one column from square matrices are required for calculating matrix cofactors, which in turn are useful for computing both the determinant and inverse of square matrices.

Let A be an m × n matrix and k an integer with 0 < k ≤ m, and k ≤ n.

a. Block size
b. Minor
c. Chiral
d. Homogeneity

22. A _____ is an opening in a wall that allows the passage of light and, if not closed or sealed, air and sound. _____s are usually glazed or covered in some other transparent or translucent material. _____s are held in place by frames, which prevent them from collapsing in.

a. 1-center problem
b. Window
c. 120-cell
d. 2-3 heap

23. In geometry, the _____ are a pair of special points used in describing conic sections. The four types of conic sections are the circle, parabola, ellipse, and hyperbola.

a. Boussinesq approximation
b. Heap
c. Foci
d. C-35

24. The _____ is a function in mathematics. The application of this function to a value x is written as ex. Equivalently, this can be written in the form e^x, where e is a mathematical constant, the base of the natural logarithm, which equals approximately 2.718281828, and is also known as Euler's number.

a. A chemical equation
b. Area hyperbolic functions
c. A Mathematical Theory of Communication
d. Exponential function

25. The mathematical concept of a _____ expresses the intuitive idea of deterministic dependence between two quantities, one of which is viewed as primary and the other as secondary. A _____ then is a way to associate a unique output for each input of a specified type, for example, a real number or an element of a given set.

a. Grill
b. Coherent
c. Going up
d. Function

26. Leonardo of Pisa (c. 1170 - c. 1250), also known as Leonardo Pisano, Leonardo Bonacci, Leonardo _____, or, most commonly, simply _____, was an Italian mathematician, considered by some 'the most talented mathematician of the Middle Ages'.

a. Fibonacci
c. Ralph C. Merkle
b. Harry Hinsley
d. Guido Castelnuovo

27. In mathematics, a _____ is a system which is not linear. Less technically, a _____ is any problem where the variabl to be solved for cannot be written as a linear sum of independent components. A nonhomogenous system, which is linear apart from the presence of a function of the independent variables, is nonlinear according to a strict definition, but such systems are usually studied alongside linear systems, because they can be transformed to a linear system as long as a particular solution is known.

a. Metric system
c. 1-center problem
b. George Dantzig
d. Nonlinear system

28. In linear algebra, _____ is an efficient algorithm for solving systems of linear equations, finding the rank of a matrix, and calculating the inverse of an invertible square matrix. _____ is named after German mathematician and scientist Carl Friedrich Gauss.

Elementary row operations are used to reduce a matrix to row echelon form.

a. Crout matrix decomposition
c. Conjugate gradient method
b. Cholesky decomposition
d. Gaussian elimination

29. The _____ is a unit of plane angle, equal to 180/π degrees, or about 57.2958 degrees. It is the standard unit of angular measurement in all areas of mathematics beyond the elementary level.

The _____ is represented by the symbol 'rad' or, more rarely, by the superscript c.

a. 120-cell
c. 1-center problem
b. 2-3 heap
d. RADIAN

30. In statistics, the _____ is the value that occurs the most frequently in a data set or a probability distribution. In some fields, notably education, sample data are often called scores, and the sample _____ is known as the modal score.

Like the statistical mean and the median, the _____ is a way of capturing important information about a random variable or a population in a single quantity.

a. Field
c. Function
b. Deltoid
d. Mode

Chapter 11. Sequences, Series, and Combinatorics

1. Leonardo of Pisa (c. 1170 - c. 1250), also known as Leonardo Pisano, Leonardo Bonacci, Leonardo _____, or, most commonly, simply _____, was an Italian mathematician, considered by some 'the most talented mathematician of the Middle Ages'.
   - a. Ralph C. Merkle
   - b. Guido Castelnuovo
   - c. Harry Hinsley
   - d. Fibonacci

2. The mathematical concept of a _____ expresses the intuitive idea of deterministic dependence between two quantities, one of which is viewed as primary and the other as secondary. A _____ then is a way to associate a unique output for each input of a specified type, for example, a real number or an element of a given set.
   - a. Going up
   - b. Grill
   - c. Coherent
   - d. Function

3. A more formal definition of a finite sequence with terms in a set S is a function from {1, 2, ..., n} to S for some n ≥ 0. An _____ in S is a function from {1, 2, ...} (the set of natural numbers without 0) to S.

   Sequences may also start from 0, so the first term in the sequence is then a_0.

   - a. Infinite sequence
   - b. A posteriori
   - c. A Mathematical Theory of Communication
   - d. A chemical equation

4. In mathematics, a _____ on a fiber bundle is a device that defines a notion of parallel transport on the bundle; that is, a way to 'connect' or identify fibers over nearby points. If the fiber bundle is a vector bundle, then the notion of parallel transport is required to be linear. Such a _____ is equivalently specified by a covariant derivative, which is an operator that can differentiate sections of that bundle along tangent directions in the base manifold.
   - a. 1-center problem
   - b. Connectivity
   - c. 120-cell
   - d. Connection

5. The _____ is a unit of plane angle, equal to 180/π degrees, or about 57.2958 degrees. It is the standard unit of angular measurement in all areas of mathematics beyond the elementary level.

   The _____ is represented by the symbol 'rad' or, more rarely, by the superscript c.

   - a. 1-center problem
   - b. 2-3 heap
   - c. 120-cell
   - d. RADIAN

6. In statistics, the _____ is the value that occurs the most frequently in a data set or a probability distribution. In some fields, notably education, sample data are often called scores, and the sample _____ is known as the modal score.

   Like the statistical mean and the median, the _____ is a way of capturing important information about a random variable or a population in a single quantity.

   - a. Deltoid
   - b. Field
   - c. Function
   - d. Mode

Chapter 11. Sequences, Series, and Combinatorics

7. The sum of an _____ $a_0 + a_1 + a_2 + …$ is the limit of the sequence of partial sums

$$S_n = a_0 + a_1 + a_2 + \cdots + a_n,$$

as $n \to \infty$, if that limit exists. If the limit exists and is finite, the series is said to converge; if it is infinite or does not exist, the series is said to diverge.

The easiest way that an _____ can converge is if all the a_n are zero for n sufficiently large. Such a series can be identified with a finite sum, so it is only infinite in a trivial sense.

However, _____ of nonzero terms can also converge, which resolves the mathematical side of several of Zeno's paradoxes.

a. Archimedes' use of infinitesimals
b. Interpolation
c. Uniform convergence
d. Infinite series

8. Call S_N the _____ to N of the sequence $\{a_n\}$, or _____ of the series. A series is the sequence of _____ s, $\{S_N\}$.

When talking about series, one can refer either to the sequence $\{S_N\}$ of the _____ s, or to the sum of the series,

$$\sum_{n=0}^{\infty} a_n$$

i.e., the limit of the sequence of _____ s - it is clear which one is meant from context.

a. Calculus
b. Partial sum
c. Binomial series
d. Hyperbolic angle

9. In mathematics, a _____ is often represented as the sum of a sequence of terms. That is, a _____ is represented as a list of numbers with addition operations between them, for example this arithmetic sequence:

1 + 2 + 3 + 4 + 5 + ... + 99 + 100

In most cases of interest the terms of the sequence are produced according to a certain rule, such as by a formula, by an algorithm, by a sequence of measurements, or even by a random number generator.

a. Concavity
b. Blind
c. Contact
d. Series

10. In mathematics, an arithmetic progression or _____ is a sequence of numbers such that the difference of any two successive members of the sequence is a constant. For instance, the sequence 3, 5, 7, 9, 11, 13... is an arithmetic progression with common difference 2.

a. Arithmetic sequence
b. Alternating series test
c. Eisenstein series
d. Edgeworth series

11. In elementary algebra, a _____ is a polynomial with two terms: the sum of two monomials. It is the simplest kind of polynomial except for a monomial.

The _____ $a^2 - b^2$ can be factored as the product of two other _____s:

$a^2 - b^2$.

The product of a pair of linear _____s a x + b and c x + d is:

2 +x + bd.

A _____ raised to the nth power, represented as

n

can be expanded by means of the _____ theorem or, equivalently, using Pascal's triangle.

a. Cylindrical algebraic decomposition
b. Real structure
c. Rational root theorem
d. Binomial

12. In mathematics, the _____ $\binom{n}{k}$ is the coefficient of the x ^{k} term in the polynomial expansion of the binomial power ^{n}.

In combinatorics, $\binom{n}{k}$ is interpreted as the number of k-element subsets of an n-element set, that is the number of ways that k things can be 'chosen' from a set of n things. Hence, $\binom{n}{k}$ is often read as 'n choose k' and called the choose function of n and k.

a. Rule of product
b. Binomial coefficient
c. Dyson conjecture
d. Symbolic combinatorics

13. In mathematics, a _____ is a constant multiplicative factor of a certain object. For example, in the expression 9x^2, the _____ of x^2 is 9.

The object can be such things as a variable, a vector, a function, etc.

a. Stability radius
b. Coefficient
c. Fibonacci polynomials
d. Multivariate division algorithm

Chapter 11. Sequences, Series, and Combinatorics

14. _____ is the addition of a set of numbers; the result is their sum or total. An interim or present total of a _____ process is termed the running total. The 'numbers' to be summed may be natural numbers, complex numbers, matrices, or still more complicated objects.

   a. 120-cell
   b. 1-center problem
   c. Summation
   d. 2-3 heap

15. In mathematics, an algebraic group G contains a unique maximal normal solvable subgroup; and this subgroup is closed. Its identity component is called the _____ of G.

   a. Block size
   b. Radical
   c. Barycentric coordinates
   d. Composite

16. In mathematics and in the sciences, a _____ (plural: _____e, formulæ or _____s) is a concise way of expressing information symbolically (as in a mathematical or chemical _____), or a general relationship between quantities. One of many famous _____e is Albert Einstein's $E = mc^2$ (see special relativity).

   In mathematics, a _____ is a key to solve an equation with variables. For example, the problem of determining the volume of a sphere is one that requires a significant amount of integral calculus to solve.

   a. 2-3 heap
   b. 120-cell
   c. 1-center problem
   d. Formula

17. _____, in mathematics and computer science, is a method of defining functions in which the function being defined is applied within its own definition. The term is also used more generally to describe a process of repeating objects in a self-similar way. For instance, when the surfaces of two mirrors are almost parallel with each other the nested images that occur are a form of _____.

   a. 2-3 heap
   b. 120-cell
   c. 1-center problem
   d. Recursion

18. In mathematics, _____ and undefined are used to explain whether or not expressions have meaningful, sensible, and unambiguous values. Not all branches of mathematics come to the same conclusion.

   The following expressions are undefined in all contexts, but remarks in the analysis section may apply.

   a. Defined
   b. Toy model
   c. LHS
   d. Plugging in

19. A _____ or inductive definition is one that defines something in terms of itself, albeit in a useful way. For it to work, the definition in any given case must be well-founded, avoiding an infinite regress.

   In simple terms, the _____ is one that grows an awareness and clarity upon itself toward a conclusive end, with each recurrence contributing something new toward the end definition.

   a. Recursive definition
   b. 120-cell
   c. 1-center problem
   d. 2-3 heap

Chapter 11. Sequences, Series, and Combinatorics

20. In mathematics and statistics, the _____ of a list of numbers is the sum of all of the list divided by the number of items in the list. If the list is a statistical population, then the mean of that population is called a population mean. If the list is a statistical sample, we call the resulting statistic a sample mean.

   a. Interval estimation
   b. Unsolved problems in statistics
   c. Analysis of variance
   d. Arithmetic mean

21. In mathematics, an _____, or central tendency of a data set refers to a measure of the 'middle' or 'expected' value of the data set. There are many different descriptive statistics that can be chosen as a measurement of the central tendency of the data items.

   An _____ is a single value that is meant to typify a list of values.

   a. A chemical equation
   b. A posteriori
   c. A Mathematical Theory of Communication
   d. Average

22. In accounting, _____ or carrying value is the value of an asset or according to its balance sheet account balance. For assets, the value is based on the original cost of the asset less any depreciation, amortization or impairment costs made against the asset. A company's _____ is its total assets minus intangible assets and liabilities.

   a. 1-center problem
   b. Depreciation
   c. 120-cell
   d. Book value

23. _____ is a term used in accounting, economics and finance to spread the cost of an asset over the span of several years.

   In simple words we can say that _____ is the reduction in the value of an asset due to usage, passage of time, wear and tear, technological outdating or obsolescence, depletion or other such factors.

   In accounting, _____ is a term used to describe any method of attributing the historical or purchase cost of an asset across its useful life, roughly corresponding to normal wear and tear.

   a. Depreciation
   b. 120-cell
   c. 1-center problem
   d. Gross sales

24. In statistics, _____ has two related meanings:

   - the arithmetic _____.
   - the expected value of a random variable, which is also called the population _____.

   It is sometimes stated that the '_____' _____s average. This is incorrect if '_____' is taken in the specific sense of 'arithmetic _____' as there are different types of averages: the _____, median, and mode. For instance, average house prices almost always use the median value for the average.

   For a real-valued random variable X, the _____ is the expectation of X.

a. Probability
b. Statistical population
c. Mean
d. Proportional hazards model

25. In mathematics, a _____ is a series with a constant ratio between successive terms. For example, the series

$$\frac{1}{2} + \frac{1}{4} + \frac{1}{8} + \frac{1}{16} + \cdots$$

is geometric, because each term is equal to half of the previous term. The sum of this series is 1, as illustrated in the following picture:

_____ are one of the simplest examples of infinite series with finite sums.

a. Telescoping series
b. Riemann series theorem
c. Summation by parts
d. Geometric series

26. In mathematics, the concept of a '_____' is used to describe the behavior of a function as its argument or input either 'gets close' to some point, or as the argument becomes arbitrarily large; or the behavior of a sequence's elements as their index increases indefinitely. _____s are used in calculus and other branches of mathematical analysis to define derivatives and continuity.

In formulas, _____ is usually abbreviated as lim.

a. Contact
b. Duality
c. Copula
d. Limit

27. _____s is the social science that studies the production, distribution, and consumption of goods and services.

The term _____s comes from the Ancient Greek oá¼°κονομῖα (oikonomia, 'management of a household, administration') from oá¼¶κος (oikos, 'house') + vÏŒμος (nomos, 'custom' or 'law'), hence 'rules of the house(hold)'.

Current _____ models developed out of the broader field of political economy in the late 19th century, owing to a desire to use an empirical approach more akin to the physical sciences.

a. A Mathematical Theory of Communication
b. Experimental economics
c. Economic
d. A chemical equation

28. In Fourier analysis, a _____ is a kind of linear operator, or transformation of functions. These operators multiply the Fourier coefficients of a function by a specified function, hence the name. Among the multipliers one can count some simple operators, such as translations and differentiation, but also some more complicated ones such as the convolutions, Hilbert transform, and others.

a. Fourier multiplier
b. Reality condition
c. Modulated complex lapped transform
d. Poisson summation formula

Chapter 11. Sequences, Series, and Combinatorics

29. In linear algebra, a _____ is a set of vectors that, in a linear combination, can represent every vector in a given vector space or free module, and such that no element of the set can be represented as a linear combination of the others. In other words, a _____ is a linearly independent spanning set. This picture illustrates the standard _____ in R^2.
    a. Chiral
    b. Dot plot
    c. Basis
    d. Conchoid

30. _____ is a method of mathematical proof typically used to establish that a given statement is true of all natural numbers. It is done by proving that the first statement in the infinite sequence of statements is true, and then proving that if any one statement in the infinite sequence of statements is true, then so is the next one.

    The method can be extended to prove statements about more general well-founded structures, such as trees; this generalization, known as structural induction, is used in mathematical logic and computer science.

    a. Finitary
    b. Ground expression
    c. Mathematical induction
    d. Herbrand structure

31. _____ is a branch of pure mathematics concerning the study of discrete objects. It is related to many other areas of mathematics, such as algebra, probability theory, ergodic theory and geometry, as well as to applied subjects in computer science and statistical physics. Aspects of _____ include 'counting' the objects satisfying certain criteria, deciding when the criteria can be met, and constructing and analyzing objects meeting the criteria, finding 'largest', 'smallest', or 'optimal' objects, and finding algebraic structures these objects may have.
    a. Restricted sumset
    b. Factorial
    c. Combinatorics
    d. Combinatorial species

32. In several fields of mathematics the term _____ is used with different but closely related meanings. They all relate to the notion of mapping the elements of a set to other elements of the same set, i.e., exchanging elements of a set.

    The general concept of _____ can be defined more formally in different contexts:

    In combinatorics, a _____ is usually understood to be a sequence containing each element from a finite set once, and only once.

    a. Cyclic permutation
    b. Linearly independent
    c. Tensor product
    d. Permutation

33. The _____ or Towers of Hanoi is a mathematical game or puzzle. It consists of three rods, and a number of disks of different sizes which can slide onto any rod. The puzzle starts with the disks neatly stacked in order of size on one rod, the smallest at the top, thus making a conical shape.
    a. Tower of Hanoi
    b. 1-center problem
    c. 2-3 heap
    d. 120-cell

34. In probability theory, an _____ is a set of outcomes to which a probability is assigned. Typically, when the sample space is finite, any subset of the sample space is an _____. However, this approach does not work well in cases where the sample space is infinite, most notably when the outcome is a real number.

a. Equaliser
c. Information set
b. Audio compression
d. Event

35. In game theory, an _____ is a set of moves or strategies taken by the players, or their payoffs resulting from the actions or strategies taken by all players. The two are complementary in that given knowledge of the set of strategies of all players, the final state of the game is known, as are any relevant payoffs. In a game where chance or a random event is involved, the _____ is not known from only the set of strategies, but is only realized when the random even are realized.
   a. Autonomous system
   c. Algebraic
   b. Equaliser
   d. Outcome

36. In set theory, a _____ is a partially ordered set such that for each $t \in T$, the set $\{s \in T : s < t\}$ is well-ordered by the relation <. For each $t \in T$, the order type of $\{s \in T : s < t\}$ is called the height of t. The height of T itself is the least ordinal greater than the height of each element of T.
   a. Set-theoretic topology
   c. Definable numbers
   b. Transitive reduction
   d. Tree

37. A _____ is a 2D geometric symbolic representation of information according to some visualization technique. Sometimes, the technique uses a 3D visualization which is then projected onto the 2D surface. The word graph is sometimes used as a synonym for _____.
   a. 120-cell
   c. 1-center problem
   b. 2-3 heap
   d. Diagram

38. In category theory, an abstract branch of mathematics, an _____ of a category C is an object I in C such that for every object X in C, there exists precisely one morphism I → X. The dual notion is that of a terminal object: T is terminal if for every object X in C there exists a single morphism X → T. _____s are also called coterminal, and terminal objects are also called final.
   a. A Mathematical Theory of Communication
   c. A posteriori
   b. A chemical equation
   d. Initial object

39. In mathematics, the _____ of a non-negative integer n, denoted by n!, is the product of all positive integers less than or equal to n. For example,

$$5! = 1 \times 2 \times 3 \times 4 \times 5 = 120$$

and
$$6! = 1 \times 2 \times 3 \times 4 \times 5 \times 6 = 720$$

The notation n! was introduced by Christian Kramp in 1808.

The _____ function is formally defined by

$$n! = \prod_{k=1}^{n} k \quad \forall n \in \mathbb{N}.$$

The above definition incorporates the instance

$$0! = 1$$

as an instance of the fact that the product of no numbers at all is 1.

a. Symbolic combinatorics
c. Partition of a set
b. Plane partition
d. Factorial

40. In computational complexity theory, an algorithm is said to take _____ if the asymptotic upper bound for the time it requires is proportional to the size of the input, which is usually denoted n.

Informally spoken, the running time increases linearly with the size of the input. For example, a procedure that adds up all elements of a list requires time proportional to the length of the list.

a. Time-constructible function
c. Truth table reduction
b. Constructible function
d. Linear time

41. In mathematics, the _____s are analogs of the ordinary trigonometric functions. The basic _____s are the hyperbolic sine 'sinh', and the hyperbolic cosine 'cosh', from which are derived the hyperbolic tangent 'tanh', etc., in analogy to the derived trigonometric functions. The inverse _____ are the area hyperbolic sine 'arsinh' (also called 'asinh', or sometimes by the misnomer of 'arcsinh') and so on.

a. Heaviside step function
c. Square root
b. Rectangular function
d. Hyperbolic function

42. In combinatorial mathematics, a _____ is an un-ordered collection of distinct elements, usually of a prescribed size and taken from a given set. Given such a set S, a _____ of elements of S is just a subset of S, where as always forsets the order of the elements is not taken into account. Also, as always forsets, no elements can be repeated more than once in a _____; this is often referred to as a 'collection without repetition'.

a. Sparsity
c. Heawood number
b. Fill-in
d. Combination

43. In mathematics, especially in set theory, a set A is a _____ of a set B if A is 'contained' inside B. Notice that A and B may coincide. The relationship of one set being a _____ of another is called inclusion.

a. Set of all sets
c. Horizontal line test
b. Cartesian product
d. Subset

44. In mathematics, an _____ or member of a set is any one of the distinct objects that make up that set.

Writing A = {1,2,3,4}, means that the _____s of the set A are the numbers 1, 2, 3 and 4. Groups of _____s of A, for example {1,2}, are subsets of A.

a. Ideal
b. Order
c. Element
d. Universal code

45. A _____ typically refers to a class of handheld calculators that are capable of plotting graphs, solving simultaneous equations, and performing numerous other tasks with variables. Most popular _____s are also programmable, allowing the user to create customized programs, typically for scientific/engineering and education applications. Due to their large displays intended for graphing, they can also accommodate several lines of text and calculations at a time.

a. Bump mapping
b. Graphing calculator
c. Support vector machines
d. Genus

46. In mathematics, the _____ of a real number is its numerical value without regard to its sign. So, for example, 3 is the _____ of both 3 and −3.

The _____ of a number a is denoted by $|a|$.

Generalizations of the _____ for real numbers occur in a wide variety of mathematical settings.

a. A chemical equation
b. Area hyperbolic functions
c. Absolute value
d. A Mathematical Theory of Communication

47. A _____ is a device for performing mathematical calculations, distinguished from a computer by having a limited problem solving ability and an interface optimized for interactive calculation rather than programming. _____s can be hardware or software, and mechanical or electronic, and are often built into devices such as PDAs or mobile phones.

Modern electronic _____s are generally small, digital, and usually inexpensive.

a. 2-3 heap
b. 120-cell
c. Calculator
d. 1-center problem

48. A _____ is one of the basic shapes of geometry: a polygon with three corners or vertices and three sides or edges which are line segments. A _____ with vertices A, B, and C is denoted ABC.

In Euclidean geometry any three non-collinear points determine a unique _____ and a unique plane.

a. Kepler triangle
b. Fuhrmann circle
c. 1-center problem
d. Triangle

49. In mathematics, the _____ is an important formula giving the expansion of powers of sums. Its simplest version states that

$$(x+y)^n = \sum_{k=0}^{n} \binom{n}{k} x^{n-k} y^k \qquad (1)$$

for any real or complex numbers x and y, and any nonnegative integer n. The binomial coefficient appearing in may be defined in terms of the factorial function n!:

$$\binom{n}{k} = \frac{n!}{k!\,(n-k)!}.$$

For example, here are the cases where 2 ≤ n ≤ 5:

$$(x+y)^2 = x^2 + 2xy + y^2$$
$$(x+y)^3 = x^3 + 3x^2y + 3xy^2 + y^3$$
$$(x+y)^4 = x^4 + 4x^3y + 6x^2y^2 + 4xy^3 + y^4$$
$$(x+y)^5 = x^5 + 5x^4y + 10x^3y^2 + 10x^2y^3 + 5xy^4 + y^5.$$

Formula is valid more generally for any elements x and y of a semiring as long as xy = yx..

a. Stirling transform
b. Lah numbers
c. Hypergeometric identities
d. Binomial theorem

50. In mathematics, a _____ is a statement that can be proved on the basis of explicitly stated or previously agreed assumptions.
   a. Boolean function
   b. Theorem
   c. Disjunction introduction
   d. Logical value

51. _____ is the likelihood or chance that something is the case or will happen. Theoretical _____ is used extensively in areas such as statistics, mathematics, science and philosophy to draw conclusions about the likelihood of potential events and the underlying mechanics of complex systems.

The word _____ does not have a consistent direct definition.

   a. Discrete random variable
   b. Probability
   c. Standardized moment
   d. Statistical significance

52. In statistics, a _____ is a subset of a population. Typically, the population is very large, making a census or a complete enumeration of all the values in the population impractical or impossible. The _____ represents a subset of manageable size.

a. Boussinesq approximation
b. Duality
c. Sample
d. Dispersion

53. In probability theory, the _____ or universal _____, often denoted S, Ω of an experiment or random trial is the set of all possible outcomes. For example, if the experiment is tossing a coin, the _____ is the set {head, tail}. For tossing a single six-sided die, the _____ is {1, 2, 3, 4, 5, 6}.
   a. Markov chain
   b. Marginal distribution
   c. Martingale central limit theorem
   d. Sample space

54. In _____, the probability of many events can be determined by direct calculation In most cases, the probabilities and odds are approximations due to rounding.
   a. Poker
   b. 2-3 heap
   c. 1-center problem
   d. 120-cell

55. An angle smaller than a right angle is called an _____ (less than 90 degrees).
   a. Integral geometry
   b. Euclidean geometry
   c. Acute angle
   d. Ultraparallel theorem

56. In geometry and trigonometry, an _____ is the figure formed by two rays sharing a common endpoint, called the vertex of the _____. The magnitude of the _____ is the 'amount of rotation' that separates the two rays, and can be measured by considering the length of circular arc swept out when one ray is rotated about the vertex to coincide with the other. Where there is no possibility of confusion, the term '_____' is used interchangeably for both the geometric configuration itself and for its angular magnitude.
   a. A posteriori
   b. Angle
   c. A Mathematical Theory of Communication
   d. A chemical equation

57. In geometry and trigonometry, a _____ is defined as an angle between two straight intersecting lines of ninety degrees, or one-quarter of a circle.
   a. Right angle
   b. Sine integral
   c. Trigonometric functions
   d. Trigonometry

58. An angle equal to two right angles is called a _____ (equal to 180 degrees).
   a. Theorem
   b. Loomis-Whitney inequality
   c. Householder transformation
   d. Straight angle

59. A pair of angles are complementary if the sum of their measures add up to 90 degrees.

If the two _____ are adjacent (i.e. have a common vertex and share a side, but do not have any interior points in common) their non-shared sides form a right angle.

In Euclidean geometry, the two acute angles in a right triangle are complementary, because there are 180>° in a triangle and 90>° have been accounted for by the right angle.

   a. Conway polyhedron notation
   b. Quincunx
   c. Hypotenuse
   d. Complementary angles

Chapter 11. Sequences, Series, and Combinatorics

60. A pair of angles is _____ if their measurements add up to 180 degrees. If the two _____ angles are adjacent their non-shared sides form a straight line. The supplement of 135 would be 45.
    a. FISH
    b. Cylinder
    c. Supplementary
    d. Dense

61. In linear algebra, two n-by-n matrices A and B over the field K are called _____ if there exists an invertible n-by-n matrix P over K such that

$$P^{-1}AP = B.$$

One of the meanings of the term similarity transformation is such a transformation of a matrix A into a matrix B.

Similarity is an equivalence relation on the space of square matrices.

_____ matrices share many properties:

- rank
- determinant
- trace
- eigenvalues
- characteristic polynomial
- minimal polynomial
- elementary divisors

There are two reasons for these facts:

- two _____ matrices can be thought of as describing the same linear map, but with respect to different bases
- the map $X \mapsto P^{-1}XP$ is an automorphism of the associative algebra of all n-by-n matrices, as the one-object case of the above category of all matrices.

Because of this, for a given matrix A, one is interested in finding a simple 'normal form' B which is _____ to A -- the study of A then reduces to the study of the simpler matrix B.

   a. Coherence
   b. Similar
   c. Dense
   d. Blinding

62. In mathematics, two quantities are called _____ if they vary in such a way that one of the quantities is a constant multiple of the other, or equivalently if they have a constant ratio.
    a. 1-center problem
    b. Proportional
    c. 120-cell
    d. 2-3 heap

63. A _____ is the longest side of a right triangle, the side opposite of the right angle. The length of the _____ of a right triangle can be found using the Pythagorean theorem, which states that the square of the length of the _____ equals the sum of the squares of the lengths of the two other sides.

For example, if one of the other sides has a length of 3 meters and the other has a length of 4 m.

a. Concyclic points
b. Reflection symmetry
c. Golden angle
d. Hypotenuse

64. In a right triangle, the cathetusoriginally from the Greek word ΚÎ¬θετος, plural catheti

- 1 Generally
- 2 References
- 3 See also
- 4 External links

In a wider sense, a _____ is any line falling perpendicularly on another line or a surface. Such a line is more commonly known as a surface normal.

a. Face diagonal
b. Line segment
c. Central angle
d. Cathetus

65. In mathematics, the _____ or Pythagoras' theorem is a relation in Euclidean geometry among the three sides of a right triangle. The theorem is named after the Greek mathematician Pythagoras, who by tradition is credited with its discovery and proof, although it is often argued that knowledge of the theory predates him.. The theorem is as follows:

In any right triangle, the area of the square whose side is the hypotenuse is equal to the sum of the areas of the squares whose sides are the two legs.

a. 1-center problem
b. 120-cell
c. 2-3 heap
d. Pythagorean theorem

66. In mathematics, a _____ is, informally, an infinitely vast and infinitely thin sheet. _____s may be thought of as objects in some higher dimensional space, or they may be considered without any outside space, as in the setting of Euclidean geometry

a. Group
b. Blocking
c. Bandwidth
d. Plane

67. In mathematics, a _____ is a curve in a Euclidian plane. The most frequently studied cases are smooth _____s, and algebraic _____s.

A smooth _____ is a curve in a real Euclidian plane R^2 is a one-dimensional smooth manifold.

a. Corresponding sides
b. Plane curve
c. Subtended
d. General position

Chapter 11. Sequences, Series, and Combinatorics

68. In mathematics, the concept of a _____ tries to capture the intuitive idea of a geometrical one-dimensional and continuous object. A simple example is the circle. In everyday use of the term '_____', a straight line is not curved, but in mathematical parlance _____s include straight lines and line segments.
    a. Kappa curve
    b. Negative pedal curve
    c. Quadrifolium
    d. Curve

69. In mathematics, _____ are a method of defining a curve. A simple kinematical example is when one uses a time parameter to determine the position, velocity, and other information about a body in motion.

    Abstractly, a relation is given in the form of an equation, and it is shown also to be the image of functions from items such as R^n.

    a. Parametric equations
    b. Multipole moment
    c. Laplace operator
    d. Differential operator

70. A _____ is the curve defined by the path of a point on the edge of circular wheel as the wheel rolls along a straight line. It is an example of a roulette, a curve generated by a curve rolling on another curve.

    The _____ is the solution to the brachistochrone problem and the related tautochrone problem.

    a. Hessian curve
    b. Superformula
    c. Hippopede
    d. Cycloid

Chapter 1

1. d	2. d	3. d	4. d	5. b	6. d	7. c	8. d	9. d	10. a
11. a	12. b	13. d	14. d	15. d	16. d	17. b	18. a	19. d	20. d
21. d	22. d	23. c	24. d	25. b	26. d	27. b	28. c	29. d	30. d
31. b	32. d	33. c	34. d	35. a	36. d	37. d	38. d	39. c	40. d
41. d	42. a	43. d	44. d	45. c	46. d	47. c	48. d	49. c	50. a
51. b	52. d	53. d	54. b	55. d	56. d	57. b	58. c	59. a	60. b
61. d	62. d	63. d	64. c	65. c	66. c	67. d	68. d	69. d	70. d
71. c	72. b								

Chapter 2

1. d	2. a	3. d	4. d	5. d	6. b	7. c	8. a	9. d	10. d
11. d	12. a	13. d	14. a	15. d	16. d	17. d	18. d	19. d	20. b
21. b	22. a	23. d	24. d	25. d	26. d	27. d	28. d	29. c	30. d
31. d	32. d	33. d	34. b	35. d	36. d	37. c	38. d	39. d	40. c
41. d	42. b	43. a	44. d	45. d	46. b	47. d	48. c	49. a	50. d
51. d	52. d	53. d	54. b	55. a	56. d	57. d	58. a	59. d	60. d
61. b	62. a	63. d	64. b	65. d	66. a	67. b	68. d	69. b	70. d
71. d	72. a	73. d	74. d	75. d	76. c	77. d	78. b	79. a	80. d
81. d	82. d	83. b	84. c	85. d	86. d	87. d	88. d	89. d	90. b
91. b	92. a	93. c							

Chapter 3

1. d	2. d	3. d	4. c	5. a	6. c	7. d	8. d	9. d	10. b
11. c	12. b	13. d	14. c	15. b	16. d	17. a	18. c	19. c	20. a
21. d	22. d	23. d	24. c	25. a	26. d	27. d	28. d	29. a	30. d
31. d	32. c	33. d	34. c	35. d	36. b	37. d	38. d	39. c	40. b
41. b	42. d	43. d	44. a	45. d	46. d	47. a	48. c	49. c	50. d

Chapter 4

1. d	2. d	3. a	4. d	5. a	6. d	7. d	8. d	9. d	10. d
11. a	12. d	13. c	14. d	15. d	16. d	17. d	18. b	19. d	20. d
21. a	22. d	23. a	24. d	25. a	26. c	27. d	28. d	29. b	30. b
31. c	32. d	33. a	34. c	35. d	36. b	37. b	38. c	39. a	40. d
41. a	42. d	43. a	44. d						

Chapter 5

1. b	2. d	3. d	4. d	5. d	6. c	7. d	8. b	9. c	10. d
11. a	12. c	13. b	14. b	15. d	16. c	17. c	18. d	19. d	20. d
21. a	22. d	23. a	24. b	25. d	26. b	27. d	28. d	29. d	30. b
31. c	32. d	33. c	34. b	35. d	36. d	37. d	38. d	39. a	40. d
41. a	42. d	43. b	44. d	45. a	46. a	47. d	48. c	49. d	50. d

ANSWER KEY

Chapter 6

1. a	2. d	3. d	4. c	5. c	6. d	7. a	8. a	9. d	10. d
11. a	12. a	13. c	14. a	15. d	16. d	17. b	18. c	19. c	20. d
21. a	22. d	23. d	24. d	25. d	26. d	27. b	28. d	29. d	30. c
31. a	32. d	33. b	34. d	35. d	36. c	37. b	38. a	39. a	40. d
41. b	42. c	43. c	44. b	45. b					

Chapter 7

1. c	2. c	3. d	4. b	5. d	6. d	7. a	8. b	9. d	10. d
11. d	12. d	13. d	14. d	15. c	16. a	17. d	18. a	19. d	20. b
21. b	22. d	23. a	24. a						

Chapter 8

1. d	2. a	3. c	4. d	5. b	6. c	7. c	8. d	9. d	10. a
11. d	12. d	13. d	14. d	15. a	16. b	17. c	18. d	19. d	20. d
21. b	22. d	23. b	24. d	25. c	26. d	27. d	28. d	29. b	30. d
31. b	32. d	33. a	34. d	35. d	36. d	37. d	38. d	39. d	40. d
41. c	42. d	43. d	44. d	45. b	46. c	47. a	48. b	49. a	50. d

Chapter 9

1. d	2. d	3. d	4. b	5. d	6. d	7. d	8. b	9. d	10. d
11. b	12. a	13. d	14. c	15. d	16. b	17. a	18. d	19. d	20. d
21. c	22. d	23. b	24. b	25. d	26. d	27. b	28. a	29. d	30. d
31. a	32. b	33. d	34. d	35. d	36. c	37. d	38. c	39. d	40. b
41. c	42. d	43. c	44. d	45. d	46. d	47. d	48. d	49. c	50. b
51. d									

Chapter 10

1. b	2. b	3. b	4. b	5. d	6. a	7. a	8. c	9. d	10. b
11. d	12. b	13. d	14. d	15. d	16. d	17. d	18. d	19. a	20. d
21. b	22. b	23. c	24. d	25. d	26. a	27. d	28. d	29. d	30. d

Chapter 11

1. d	2. d	3. a	4. d	5. d	6. d	7. d	8. b	9. d	10. a
11. d	12. b	13. b	14. c	15. b	16. d	17. d	18. a	19. a	20. d
21. d	22. d	23. a	24. c	25. d	26. d	27. c	28. a	29. c	30. c
31. c	32. d	33. a	34. d	35. d	36. d	37. d	38. d	39. d	40. d
41. d	42. d	43. d	44. c	45. b	46. c	47. c	48. d	49. d	50. b
51. b	52. c	53. d	54. a	55. c	56. b	57. a	58. d	59. d	60. c
61. b	62. b	63. d	64. d	65. d	66. d	67. b	68. d	69. a	70. d

www.ingramcontent.com/pod-product-compliance
Lightning Source LLC
Chambersburg PA
CBHW082046230426

43670CB00016B/2789